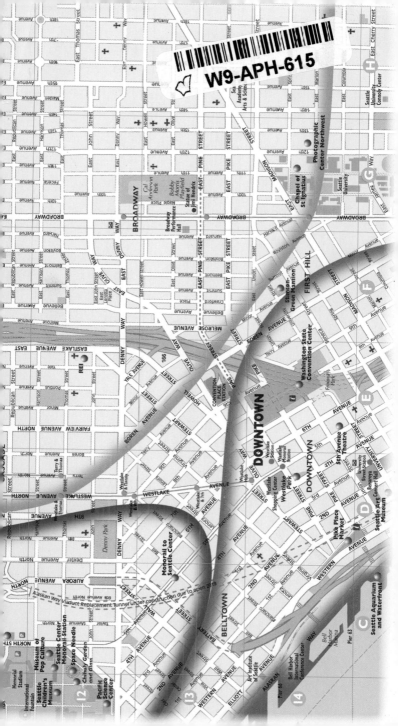

Fodor's
25Best

SEATTLE

How to Use
This Book

KEY TO SYMBOLS	
✚ Map reference to the accompanying fold-out map	🛥 Nearest riverboat or ferry stop
✉ Address	♿ Facilities for visitors with disabilities
☎ Telephone number	❓ Other practical information
🕐 Opening/closing times	▷ Further information
🍴 Restaurant or café	ℹ Tourist information
🚊 Nearest rail station	✋ Admission charges:
🚌 Nearest bus route	Expensive (more than $17) Moderate ($10–$17) Inexpensive ($9 or less)

This guide is divided into four sections
● **Essential Seattle:** An introduction to the city and tips on making the most of your stay.
● **Seattle by Area:** We've broken the city into six areas, and recommended the best sights, shops, entertainment venues, nightlife and where to eat in each one. Suggested walks help you to explore on foot.
● **Where to Stay:** The best hotels, whether you're looking for luxury, budget or something in between.
● **Need to Know:** The info you need to make your trip run smoothly, including getting about by public transportation, weather tips, emergency phone numbers and useful websites.

Navigation In the Seattle by Area chapter, we've given each area its own color, which is also used on the locator maps throughout the book and the map on the inside front cover.

Maps The fold-out map with this book is a comprehensive street plan of Seattle. The grid on this fold-out map is the same as the grid on the locator maps within the book. We've given grid references within the book for each sight and listing.

Contents

Introducing Seattle

When the Cordilleran Ice Sheet of North America began to retreat 14,000 years ago, it left behind the vast Puget Sound. Now a fjord of flooded glacial valleys, it has Seattle at its helm—the Emerald City surrounded by many deep shades of green.

Yet amongst such stunning natural beauty, Seattle, named after the Native American Chief Seattle, whose people lived here for thousands of years before the first Europeans arrived in the late 1700s, is built on industry and technology. First as a timber town, then subsequently as a shipbuilding center during the Klondike Gold Rush of the 1890s. During WWII, the city served as the aircraft manufacturing headquarters for Boeing. Then, later, in the 1980s, Microsoft moved in, followed by Amazon and other tech companies.

Today, Seattle, with its 700,000 residents, is one of the fastest-growing big cities in the US, adding to an already high real-estate market. The city's famed music scene, which rose to international prominence thanks to forefathers like Jimi Hendrix,

Nirvana and Pearl Jam, still pushes the envelope. The city is the birthplace of grunge music—alternative rock with a hint of punk and heavy metal that emerged in the late 80s. With local bands Nirvana, Pearl Jam, Soundgarden and Alice in Chains all releasing hugely successful albums in the 1990s, grunge became mainstream on a global scale. Seattle's Sub Pop was one of the leading independent record labels of that time, and as grunge waned, Sub Pop held on, and is still in business today with its headquarters Downtown.

The city also has a vibrant fine arts community, while craft beer, single-origin coffee, and fresh local seafood fill the innovative drink and food scene. And outdoor enthusiasts have but to look to any direction to draw inspiration for their next kayaking, mountain biking or hiking adventure.

FACTS AND FIGURES

- Estimated visitors in 2015: 38 million
- Seattle has about 150 rainy days a year.
- Seattle is ranked one of the most literate cities in the US, and over 60 percent of residents have a college degree or higher.
- Seattle is the fastest-growing big city in the USA, with 57 people arriving every day.
- There are more dogs than children in Seattle: about 170,000 dogs to 120,000 kids.

MOUNTAINS UPON MOUNTAINS

Seattle sits between two soaring mountain ranges. The Cascade Mountains lie to the east of the city—dominated by snowcapped Mt. Baker—while the sawlike ridges of the Olympic Range frame the western sky. Both ranges can be seen from many neighborhoods in the city, but the best views can be found on the affluent Queen Anne Hill, northwest of Downtown.

CITY OF WATER

Seattle is between two significant bodies of water. To the west is Puget Sound, a sprawling arm of the Pacific Ocean that reaches all the way from Whidbey Island, 30 miles (48km) north of Seattle, to Olympia, 50 miles (80km) south of Seattle. To the east is Lake Washington, one of the country's largest urban lakes.

BIRTHPLACE OF THE BEAN

In 1971, three local entrepreneurs opened a small coffeehouse just below the Pike Place Market. They named their shop after a caffeine-crazed first mate in Melville's *Moby Dick*: Starbucks. Their venture has since become the largest coffeehouse company in the world, with more than 25,000 locations across the globe.

A Short Stay in Seattle

DAY 1

Morning Take a taxi to Queen Anne Hill, a historic (and gorgeous) neighborhood north of Downtown. The hill is one of the city's tallest—its summit is 456ft (139m) above Puget Sound. Stop in for a hearty breakfast at the **5 Spot** café (▷ 56), hit the shops on Queen Anne Avenue, and don't miss the stellar Downtown views from **Kerry Park Viewpoint** (▷ 53).

Mid-morning Walk along the waterfront, basking in the cool sea breeze that wafts off Elliott Bay. Stop in at the **Seattle Aquarium** (▷ 29), with exhibits featuring shorebirds, six-gill sharks, tide pools and cute sea otters.

Lunch Hop on the **Bainbridge Island Ferry** (▷ 25) to Winslow, a can't-miss 35-minute ride across Puget Sound. Stroll Winslow's quaint boulevards and lunch on great fish-and-chips at the Harbor Public House.

Afternoon Upon returning to Seattle's Colman Dock, walk eastward up the Harbor Steps into **Downtown** Seattle (▷ 36) proper. Visit the stunning **Seattle Art Museum** (▷ 30–31) before heading toward the "retail core," a four-block goldmine of high-end shops and department stores that surround Pine Street, between 5th and 7th avenues.

Dinner Cash in on your early planning by being on time for your reservation at **Loulay** (▷ 43), where chef Thierry Rautureau adds his magic to a menu driven by the finest local ingredients—without breaking the bank. Start with crispy crab beignets, followed by a succulent steak smothered in peppercorn sauce.

Evening Walk south along 1st Avenue toward **Pioneer Square** (▷ 28) and its mind-boggling array of bars and lounges, many of which feature live music nightly.

DAY 2

Morning Ride Seattle's **Monorail** (▷ 53) then use the city bus system—which is renowned for its ecoconscious hybrid and electrically powered vehicles—to get to the leafy neighborhood of Madrona, east of Downtown. Have breakfast at another popular spot: the Hi Spot Café, home to some of the city's best fresh-baked scones.

Mid-morning Explore the **Washington Park Arboretum** (▷ 64–65), a 230-acre (93ha) oasis of botanical diversity in Seattle's Montlake neighborhood. The Arboretum, which is maintained by the nearby **University of Washington** (▷ 77), has one of North America's largest collections of maple and sorbus trees, along with a renowned Japanese Garden.

Lunch If the weather cooperates, enjoy an outdoor lunch at **Agua Verde** (▷ 82), a standout Mexican-inspired eatery on the shores of Portage Bay.

Afternoon Walk north from Agua Verde along **University Way** (▷ 77), the cultural and culinary hub of the University of Washington. Shop for vintage clothing and unique gifts along the way before visiting the university's **Henry Art Gallery** (▷ 76). Travel to **Capitol Hill** (▷ 60–61), the bustling nexus of Seattle's artistic community. This area is loaded with funky boutiques, preeminent bistros and nightclubs. Stroll along **Broadway** (▷ 60), which provides the heartbeat of the city's cultural life.

Dinner Stop in at one of Capitol Hill's incredible restaurants—**Nue** and **Café Presse** (▷ 70) rank among the best.

Evening Head down the hill into Downtown and catch a show at Benaroya Hall, home to the Seattle Symphony. Or head north to Seattle Center for a performance by the **Seattle Opera** (▷ 55) in McCaw Hall.

These pages are a quick guide to the Top 25, which are described in more detail later. Here they are listed alphabetically, and the tinted background shows which area they are in.

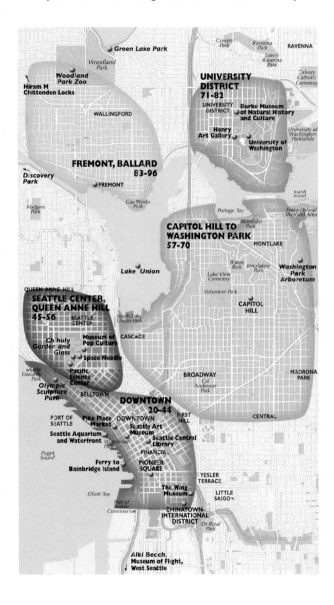

Green Lake Park

Woodland Park

Woodland Park Zoo

Hiram M Chittenden Locks

Cowen Park

Ravenna Park

RAVENNA

Lower Ravenna Park

Calvary Catholic Cemetery

UNIVERSITY DISTRICT 71–82

UNIVERSITY DISTRICT

Burke Museum of Natural History and Culture

WALLINGFORD

Henry Art Gallery

University of Washington

University of Washington Parklands

FREMONT, BALLARD 83–96

Discovery Park

FREMONT

Rodgers Park

Gas Works Park

Portage Bay

Marsh Island

Foster Island Wetland Area

CAPITOL HILL TO WASHINGTON PARK 57–70

Montlake Park

MONTLAKE

Boren Park

Interlaken Park

Washington Park Arboretum

Lake Union

Lake View Cemetery

Volunteer Park

QUEEN ANNE HILL

SEATTLE CENTER, QUEEN ANNE HILL 45–56

SEATTLE CENTER

South Lake Union Park

CASCADE

CAPITOL HILL

Chihuly Garden and Glass

Museum of Pop Culture

Myrtle Edwards Park

Space Needle

Pacific Science Center

Olympic Sculpture Park

BELLTOWN

BROADWAY

Cal Anderson Park

MADRONA PARK

DOWNTOWN 20–44

DOWNTOWN

FIRST HILL

CENTRAL

PORT OF SEATTLE

Pike Place Market

Seattle Art Museum

Seattle Aquarium and Waterfront

Waterfront Park

Seattle Central Library

FINANCIAL

Puget Sound

Ferry to Bainbridge Island

PIONEER SQUARE

YESLER TERRACE

Elliott Bay

The Wing Museum

LITTLE SAIGON

Port of Seattle Commission

CHINATOWN-INTERNATIONAL DISTRICT

Dr Rizal Park

Alki Beach, Museum of Flight, West Seattle

ESSENTIAL SEATTLE TOP 25

9

Shopping

Independent shops selling books, maps and vintage clothing manage well here in Seattle, even amongst the big brand department stores. There's surely something for everyone, whether it's a memorable souvenir, a piece of local art, or a unique curio from the other side of the world.

Pike Place Market

For small gifts, start at Pike Place Market, where farmers and artisans set up their stalls before 9am. The lower floors consist of shops that sell vintage magazines, comics, vinyl records and T-shirts. In the crafts area you'll find wood and metal items, as well as pottery, jewelry, textiles, and regional food items like preserves, dried cherries and smoked fish.

Sample the Wares

Washington wines, having garnered top awards at international tastings, are another special purchase. Grapes are grown east of Washington's Cascade Range at the same latitude as the wine-making provinces of France—Pike Market Cellars offers a good selection. You can sample the local wines at one of the tasting rooms close to the city—try Chateau Ste. Michelle (▷ 104), 15 miles (24km) northeast of Downtown in Woodinville, Washington state's oldest winery (founded in 1934). To re-create Northwest cuisine at home, stop at one of Seattle's abundant bookstores around Pike Place Market and Pioneer Square for cookbooks penned by top local chefs like Renee Erickson and Makini Howell. Cookbooks are also

SEATTLE'S SALES TAX

When purchasing items, you'll likely find an additional 10.1 percent tax tacked on to your bill, with some exemptions such as groceries and prescription drugs. As Washington is one of only seven states without a state income tax, this retail sales tax is the state's principal tax source and the amount varies from city to city. Accommodation in Seattle has an added tax, too, which is currently at 15.6 percent.

Clockwise from top: shopping at Fisherman's Wharf; fresh produce at University District

available at the Made in Washington (▷ 38) shop, which carries only items that are made, produced or grown in the state. Seattle is well-known for its glass art, primarily through the work of Dale Chihuly and other glass-blowers working in the tradition of the Pilchuck Glass School in Stanwood (50 miles/81km north of Seattle), who exhibit and sell their brilliant wares in galleries and studios throughout the city. For the tacky and the bizarre, check out the tourist haunts along Seattle's waterfront and the shops in Fremont. For joke and novelty items, you can't beat Archie McPhee & Co. (1300 N 45th Street) in the Wallingford neighborhood.

Dedicated Shoppers

Today, to find the greatest variety of stores in a compact area head straight for the Downtown retail core, the Pike Place Market and neighboring Belltown and Pioneer Square. Due to its stunning setting and the popularity of outdoor sports, Seattle reigns as a manufacturer and retailer of such outdoor and recreational apparel. There are outfitters both Downtown and in the South Lake Union neighborhood, where REI (▷ 67) resides. Visit Downtown department stores and upscale malls like Westlake Center and Pacific Place—or check out Belltown designer boutiques along 1st and 2nd avenues from Bell Steet.

Farmers' Market; Belltown; Westlake Center; Pike Place Market by night and day

FINE ART

Seattle's fine arts galleries and craft shops are concentrated in Downtown malls, around the Seattle Art Museum and in Pioneer Square. Many feature Native American art of the Northwest Coast. You will find not only artiques—Native American baskets, jewelry, early Edward S. Curtis photographs, ceremonial masks and wood carvings—but also striking contemporary prints and carvings created by Native American artists working today. Authentic Inuit stone and bone sculptures, colorful and intricately carved Coast Salish panels, plus other First Peoples fine art can be found at the Steinbrueck Native Gallery (▷ 39) by Pike Place Market or at the Daybreak Star Arts Center (▷ 102).

Shopping by Theme

Whether you're looking for a department store, a quirky boutique, or something in between, you'll find it all in Seattle. On this page shops are listed by theme. For a more detailed write-up, see the individual listings in Seattle by Area.

Seattle by Night

After-hours entertainment in Seattle runs the gamut from classical music to spectator sports, comedy to swing dance.

Performance Arts
The Seattle Opera, Pacific Northwest Ballet, Seattle Symphony, and several theater companies are in residence between late fall and early summer. In May and June, the city hosts the Seattle International Film Festival. At any given time during the rest of the year, a half-dozen local cinemas are showing foreign or independent films. Concert venues like The Paramount Theatre (▷ 40) and the 5th Avenue Theatre (▷ 34) book touring artists all the time, and local theater companies stagger their plays so that audiences can enjoy shows every month.

Summer Nightlife
In summer, an evening of baseball is fun; when Mariners' action flags, take a minute to check out the view from Safeco Field's upper deck (▷ 41). Another pleasant option is a twilight ferry ride across Elliott Bay. Summer days are long—perfect for an evening stroll while it's still light, followed by drinks and dinner on the patio of a waterfront restaurant.

Cooler Months
On a cold winter's evening, stop for a cocktail at a swanky hotel lounge, quench your thirst at a Belltown tavern, or see what's on tap at one of Seattle's excellent brewpubs. Seattle's many clubs (▷ panel) host live music, dancing, comedy or improvisational theater.

From top: the Space Needle; Whidbey Island at sunset; Chihuly Garden and Glass

CLUBS FOR ALL
Belltown hangouts that once played grunge now feature hip-hop, while other Downtown nightclubs cater to an older, more upscale crowd that enjoys salsa dancing or listening to jazz. Pioneer Square has both stylish clubs and taverns that draw young singles. For acoustic music, head to Ballard, where the atmosphere is more laid-back. Capitol Hill along Pike and Pine is home to the city's gay bars and clubs.

Where to Eat

Naturally influenced by the fresh, local bounty of the Pacific Northwest, Seattle's restaurant scene is abound with seafood and farmers' market produce. Add to that a continued accession of residents from around the globe bringing their culinary influences, and the visitor here will experience innovative and daring cuisine.

Variety of Choice

From easy food truck options to memorable Michelin-star dining rooms and all manner of bistros in between, Seattle's food and drink scene is lively and abundant. Families will find welcoming restaurants with high-chairs, vegetarians will find no shortage of healthy meat-free dishes, and dessert lovers will rejoice at all the sweet confections available.

Seafood Central

With the city's proximity to fresh seafood, it makes sense that Seattle's seafood restaurants rank among the best in the country. In the summer months, wild Alaskan salmon is the headliner; wintertime favorites include Alaskan halibut and king crab. Plus, the local oysters and mussels are not to be missed.

When to Go

Breakfast is sometimes served all day at coffee shops and diners, but typical breakfast hours are from 7 to 11am. Lunch begins at 11am and concludes by 3pm; whereas dinner begins at 5pm and finishes at 9pm during the week and 10 or 11pm on weekends. Brunch is becoming increasingly popular in Seattle.

TAXES AND TIPPING

As with most purchases in the city of Seattle, a sales tax of 10.1 percent is added to restaurant bills; on top of that, customers are expected to add at least 15 percent gratuity. (That's assuming the meal was satisfactory, of course.) For the vast majority of diners, a 20 percent tip is standard—especially at the city's upscale eateries.

From top: Pacific Place; Seattle is known for its seafood restaurants; Neu bistro by day and night

Where to Eat by Cuisine

There are restaurants to suit all tastes and budgets in Seattle. On this page they are listed by cuisine. For a more detailed description of each restaurant, see Seattle by Area.

Asian
FOB Poke Bar (▷ 43)
Chan (▷ 42)
Maneki (▷ 43)
Sushi Kashiba (▷ 44)
Tamarind Tree (▷ 44)
Thanh Vi (▷ 32)

Bistros
Betty (▷ 56)
Café Campagne (▷ 42)
Café Presse (▷ 70)
Crow (▷ 56)
Nue (▷ 70)
Matt's in the Market (▷ 43)
Pair (▷ 82)
Le Pichet (▷ 44)

Coffee and Pastries
Café Besalu (▷ 96)
Caffè Ladro (▷ 70)
Dahlia Bakery (▷ 42)
Elm Coffee Roasters (▷ 42)
Espresso Vivace (▷ 70)
Macrina Bakery (▷ 43)
Panama Hotel Tea & Coffee House (▷ 44)
Queen Bee Café (▷ 70)
Zeitgeist Kunst and Kaffee (▷ 44)

European
Altura (▷ 70)
Die Bierstube (▷ 82)
Il Corvo (▷ 43)
Loulay (▷ 43)
Pink Door (▷ 44)
Salumi (▷ 44)
Serafina (▷ 70)
Serious Pie (▷ 44)

Latin American
Agua Verde (▷ 82)
Arepa Venezuelan Kitchen (▷ 82)
La Carta de Oaxaca (▷ 96)
Copal (▷ 42)
Paseo Caribbean Food (▷ 96)
Tacos Chukis (▷ 56)
Tango (▷ 70)

Lebanese
Cafe Munir (▷ 96)
Mashawi (▷ 56)

Northwest/American
5 Spot (▷ 56)
Canlis (▷ 96)
Dahlia Lounge (▷ 42)
Eden Hill (▷ 56)
Farestart (▷ 43)

Hattie's Hat (▷ 96)
Jak's Grill (▷ 82)
The Metropolitan Grill (▷ 43)
Palace Kitchen (▷ 44)
Pine Box (▷ 70)
Portage Bay Café (▷ 82)
Shultzy's Sausage (▷ 82)
Skycity at the Needle (▷ 56)
Toulouse Petit (▷ 56)
Windy City Pie (▷ 56)

Seafood
The Brooklyn Seafood, Steak & Oyster Bar (▷ 42)
The Crab Pot (▷ 42)
Ivar's (▷ 43)
Jack's Fish Spot (▷ 43)
Manolin (▷ 96)
Pike Place Chowder (▷ 44)
Taylor Shellfish Farms Oyster Bar (▷ 44)
The Walrus and the Carpenter (▷ 96)

Vegetarian
Araya's Place (▷ 70)
Eggs and Plants (▷ 42)
Veggie Grill (▷ 82)

Top Tips For...

These great suggestions will help you tailor your ideal visit to Seattle, no matter how you choose to spend your time. Each suggestion has a fuller write-up elsewhere in the book.

INDULGE IN BOUTIQUE HOTELS
Stop in for an early-evening cocktail at Hotel Sorrento's (▷ 112) bar, the Fireside Room.
Relax with a glass of Washington wine at the Hotel Vintage (▷ 111), where each luxurious room is dedicated to a local vineyard or winery.
Enjoy a floor-to-ceiling view of Puget Sound and the Olympic Mountains from a room at the quaint Inn at the Market (▷ 112).

STROLLING SEATTLE'S NEIGHBORHOODS
Watch the salmon climb the fish ladder at Ballard's Hiram M. Chittenden Locks (▷ 88–89).
Go shopping on Sunday at the "Center of the Universe," also known as Fremont, at its Sunday Market (▷ 94).
Walk down Azalea Way, a verdant greenway that snakes through Washington Park Arboretum (▷ 64–65).

THEATER AND FILM
Catch an independent or foreign film at the SIFF Cinema Egyptian (▷ 69), housed in a century-old former Masonic Temple.
Admire the Seattle Opera at McCaw Hall (▷ 55), a Seattle landmark venue.
Catch a Broadway musical at the ornate 5th Avenue Theatre (▷ 34).

TOPPING UP THE WARDROBE
Try out the latest women's fashions at Les Amis in Ballard (▷ 95).
Designer menswear and impeccable service can be found at Kuhlman (▷ 38).
Stock up at Filson (▷ 37), for rugged outdoor attire that's made to last and made in Seattle.
Buy yourself some stylish footwear at The Woolly Mammoth (▷ 80) on University Way.

Clockwise from top left: Hotel Vintage; the Center of the Universe sign in Fremont;

the opulent interior of the 5th Avenue Theatre; the Founding Collection at the Frye Art Museum

SAMPLING THE BEST BISTROS

Sample small-plate heaven at Nue (▷ 70), where you can eat your way around the world in one sitting.

Bask in the warm glow of Altura (▷ 70), which specializes in Italian cuisine.

Escape to Paris in Café Campagne (▷ 42), a masterful combination of romantic atmosphere and gourmet French cuisine.

LIVING THE HIGH LIFE

Dine at Canlis (▷ 96), the city's undisputed champion of high cuisine. The views, the food and the service are exemplary.

Stay at Hotel Max (▷ 110), one of the city's finest hotels, which has colorful rooms filled with local art, and special treats and services for pets.

Get a bird's-eye view of the city and its fabulous coastal setting with a scenic flight by seaplane from Lake Union (▷ 62).

BRINGING THE KIDS

Science is hands-on at the Pacific Science Center (▷ 50–51), a family favorite.

Go to the top of the Space Needle (▷ 52). This legendary structure retains every bit of its space-age appeal.

Take them shopping at one of the city's specialty shops, such as the Market Magic Shop (▷ 38).

Get up close and personal with the local wildlife at the Seattle Aquarium (▷ 29).

DOING WHAT'S FREE

Gaze at the Stars at the University of Washington Observatory (▷ 81).

Go for a Sunday Public Sail at the Center for Wooden Boats (▷ 62).

Enjoy an hour-long ride on Lake Union with volunteer crew members (▷ 62).

Cool off on a warm day at the International Fountain at the Seattle Center.

Let off some steam at the Green Lake Park playground (▷ 86–87).

EXPLORING ESPRESSO AND TEA

Grab a steaming cappuccino at the modern and bright Elm Coffee Roasters café (▷ 42).

Buy yourself some beans at Caffè Ladro (▷ 70), which sells fantastic java.

Soak up the vibe while you sip at the sidewalk café, Espresso Vivace (▷ 70).

Enjoy a 40-minute Japanese Tea Ceremony in Washington Park Arboretum (▷ 64–65).

Take in local art on the exposed brick walls while you drink your expresso at Zeitgeist Kunst and Kaffee (▷ 44).

DANCING INTO THE NIGHT

Go where the dancers are: Pioneer Square (▷ 28), packed with bars, dance clubs and pool halls.

Whoop it up in Belltown (▷ 13) at any one of the swanky clubs and cocktail lounges.

Get down with the youngsters on Capitol Hill (▷ 60–61), Seattle's most liberal neighborhood.

WATERFRONT WALKS

Take in the significance of the landing site at Alki Beach (▷ 100) and visit a small replica of the Statue of Liberty.

Check out the Historic Ships Wharf at Lake Union (▷ 62) and let the kids splash at the spraypark in the summer.

Peek in the tidal pools and enjoy the wide vistas at Discovery Park (▷ 102).

Amble through modern art at the Olympic Sculpture Park with views overlooking Puget Sound (▷ 26).

THE SPORTING LIFE

Try to catch a baseball game during the summertime at Safeco Field (▷ 41), home of the Major League Mariners.

Rent a bright green bike for the day (▷ panel, 81) and explore the network of cycle routes and multi-use trails around the city.

Shop for outdoor gear at REI (▷ 67), the largest outdoor equipment retailer in town.

From top: Joining friends for a drink; replica of the Statue of Liberty at Alki Beach; Safeco Field

Seattle by Area

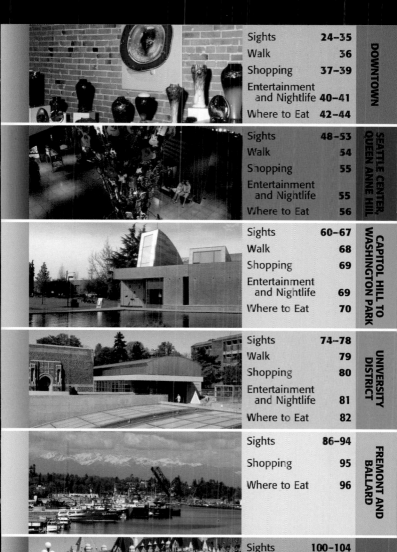

Although it has always been the beating heart of Seattle's economy, Downtown is also home to cultural treasures. Here you'll find a lively market, top museums and galleries, and wonderful eateries.

11

12

WEST WESTERN AVENUE
WEST ELLIOTT AVENUE

Myrtle Edwards Park

Eagle Street

Broad Street

Olympic Sculpture Park

Clay Street

1st Avenue

Cedar Street

Vine Street

Wall Street

2ND AVENUE

13

Victoria BC, San Juan Islands

Pier 70

WESTERN AVENUE

ELLIOTT AVENUE

BATTERY STREET

BELLTOWN

4TH AVENUE

5th Avenue

Pier 69 Victoria Clipper Ferry Dock

ALASKAN WAY

Art Institute of Seattle

Bell Street

Blanchard Street

1st Avenue

2ND AVENUE

3rd Avenue

Alaskan Way Viaduct Replacement—State Route 99 Tunnel construction (due to open 2016)

14

Pier 67

Pier 66

Bell Harbor International Conference Center

Lenora Avenue

Virginia Avenue

Steinbrueck Native Gallery

WESTERN AVENUE

STEWART

PORT OF SEATTLE

Bell Harbor Marina

Pier 63

Pier 62

Pike Place Market

ALASKAN WAY

Seattle Aquarium and Waterfront

Harbor Steps

Puget Sound

Waterfront Park

Pier 57

ALASKAN WAY

15

Seattle Great Wheel

Pier 56

Pier 55

Pier 54

Ye Olde Curiosity Shop & Museum

Pier 53

Puget Sound Islands

Ferry to Bainbridge Island

Pier 52

16

Pier 48

| 0 | | 250 m |
| 0 | | 250 yds |

Elliott Bay

17

A   **B**   **C**   **D**

Chinatown-International District

Eating out is one of the chief pleasures of Seattle's colorful Chinatown

THE BASICS

cidbia.org

F17

Between S Main and Lane streets and 5th and 8th avenues S; "Little Saigon" 12th Avenue S and Jackson Street

Central Link: International District-Chinatown

HIGHLIGHTS

● The Wing Museum (▷ 33)
● The Seattle Pinball Museum
● Uwajimaya, a large Asian emporium
● Fuji Bakery for Japanese-French pastries
● Hing Hay Park with its ornate Grand Pavilion

TIPS

● For fans of karaoke, head to Venus Karaoke on South King Street for a Korean-style karaoke experience.
● Daiso on 6th Avenue South is a great budget option for Japanese gifts.

Situated just south of the Downtown core, the Chinatown-International District (CID) is one of Seattle's oldest neighborhoods. Dotted with historical landmarks, fascinating museums and diverse lunch options, visitors will undoubtedly enjoy exploring this vibrant ethnic community.

Three in one Comprised of three smaller individual areas—Chinatown, Japantown and Little Saigon—the CID neighborhood saw its first Chinese immigrant workers in the 1860s. Followed by the arrival of other migrants, including the Japanese, Vietnamese, Filipino and African Americans, this area quickly began to reflect its residents' origins, which is reflected in its cuisine. The delicious culinary options here include authentic Chinese noodles, Japanese sushi, Vietnamese pho and Thai curries.

Architectural buffs You'll appreciate the surprising number of intact pre-WWII red-brick buildings on each block, mixed with the traditional Chinese pagodas and tile-roofed balconies. Interesting too, is the little Kobe Terrace park featuring a four-ton, 200-year-old Yukimidoro stone lantern gifted by Seattle's sister city, Kobe, Japan.

Soak it up The six-story Panama Hotel (▷ 109) on South Main Street, built in 1910, contains the last remaining Japanese bathhouse in the country. The hotel offers tours, and mochi (Japanese rice cakes) in its café (▷ 44).

The Bainbridge Island ferry (right) is one of several that ply the Sound (below)

Ferry to Bainbridge Island

There's nothing more delightful than catching a Washington State ferry to Bainbridge Island. Standing at the stern as the boat pulls away from Colman Dock, you can see the entire Seattle skyline unfold.

The ferry It takes 35 minutes to get to Bainbridge Island from the Downtown waterfront. En route, you can look back to see an amazing panorama: the Seattle cityscape and Mt. Rainier to the east, and Bainbridge Island and snow-capped Olympic Range to the west.

Touring on foot Once you disembark at the Bainbridge ferry dock, walk the short distance to the town of Winslow, visit the charming boutiques, browse at Eagle Harbor Books, stop for lunch at Hitchcock Deli or order treats from the Blackbird Bakery. If it's Saturday (Apr to mid-Dec), catch the market on the Winslow green, or visit Bainbridge's Island Winery for tasting Thu–Mon. If you're synchronizing your return with the sunset, you could linger on the waterfront deck at The Harbour Public House.

Touring by car or bike If you have wheels, visit Bloedel Reserve and walk the trails. Continuing across Agate Pass Bridge on to the Kitsap Peninsula, you enter Port Madison Indian Reservation and the town of Suquamish, where leader Chief Sealth is buried. The Suquamish Museum gives an interesting insight into the tribe's history.

THE BASICS

Bainbridge Ferry
wsdot.wa.gov/ferries
🔲 D16
✉ Colman Dock, pier 52; 801 Alaskan Way
☎ 206/464-6-00, 888/808-7977
🕐 From Seattle, 6.10am–2.10am; from Bainbridge, last ferry at 1.25am
🚆 Central Link to Pioneer Square
🚌 RapidRide C Line
💵 Inexpensive

Bainbridge Vineyards
bainbridgevineyards.com
✉ 8989 NE Day Road
☎ 206/842-9463
🕐 Tasting Thu–Mon 12–5. Tours some weekends

Bloedel Reserve
bloedelreserve.org
✉ 7521 NE Dolphin Drive
☎ 206/842-7531
🕐 Jun–Aug Tue–Wed 10–4, Thu–Sun 10–6; Sep–May Tue–Sun 10–4
💵 Moderate

Olympic Sculpture Park

TOP 25

Modern art along the waterfront, including Echo (below right)

THE BASICS

seattleartmuseum.org

➕ B13

✉ 2902 Western Avenue

☎ 206/654-3100

🕐 Half hour before dawn to half hour after dusk

🍴 La Panaderia, open Nov–Feb, Sat–Sun 10–3, Mar–Oct, daily 10–3

🚌 1, 2, 13, 15, 18, 21, 22

♿ Free

♿ Very good

HIGHLIGHTS

● *Echo*
● *Eagle*
● Wandering among the curved forms of *Wake*, by Richard Serra
● *Seattle Cloud Cover*, on the footbridge, by Teresita Fernandez
● Viewing exhibits with the sunset as a backdrop

TIPS

● There are great photo opportunities of the Seattle skyline and Elliott Bay.
● It's just a 10-minute walk from the Space Needle, and 20 minutes from Pike Place.

Some of the Seattle Art Museum's most monumental sculptural works have been brought outdoors in this urban waterfront park, transforming a former industrial wasteland into an open-air gallery with stunning views of the Olympic Mountains, Puget Sound and Space Needle.

Birth of the park The idea for the park was born in the late 1990s, and finally came to fruition in 2007, thanks to a gift of $30 million from Mary and Jon Shirley, the latter a former president of Microsoft.

Innovative art One of the most prominent works in the collection is the pale, slender and dramatic 46ft (14m) tall *Echo*, by Spanish artist Jaume Plensa, installed in 2014. In the form of an elongated head, it towers over the entire waterfront. Other stand-out exhibits include the elegant, bright-red *Eagle* by American sculptor Alexander Calder, and Mark di Suvero's *Schubert Sonata*, its welded metal curves highlighted by passing clouds. Also check out the fun series, *Eye Benches*, by Louise Bourgeois.

Neukom Vivarium American artist Mark Dion was commissioned by the Seattle Art Museum to create this mixed-media installation, which includes a greenhouse that contains the exhibit's elements of sculpture, horticulture and the environment. Central to the piece is a decaying tree, showing how it transforms and provides a habitat for insects, plants and bacteria.

To many residents, Pike Place Market is Seattle's heart and soul. Here, people of every background converge, from city professionals and farmers to craftspeople and tourists.

Farmers' market Pike Place Market was founded in 1907 so that farmers could sell directly to the consumer. It was an immediate success until its decline in World War II. Threatened by demolition in the 1960s, it underwent renovation in 2012, and expanded in 2017 with the MarketFront site.

Feast for the senses The three-block area stretching between Pike and Virginia has flower-stalls, fishsellers, produce displays, tea shops, bakeries, herbal apothecaries, magic stores and much more. Street musicians play Peruvian panpipes or sing the blues, and the fragrance of flowers and fresh bread fills the air.

Exploring the market Before you begin, pick up a map from the information booth (1st Avenue and Pike Street, near the big clock) and head out from the bronze sculpture of Rachel the pig. Watch out for the flying fish (at Pike Place Fish), stop to admire the artfully arranged produce and flower displays, and enjoy the handmade items in the crafts area. Be sure to visit one of the earliest Starbucks at 1912 Pike Place. The shop opened in 1976, but it was actually the business's second location; the first store was opened in 1971 on Western Avenue.

THE BASICS

pikeplacemarket.org

D14

Between 1st Avenue and Western Avenue, Pike Street and Virginia Street

206/682-7453

Merchants daily 10–6, fresh produce from 7am, restaurants 6am–1.30am. Closed Christmas and Thanksgiving

Many buses including Route 10 on Pine and 1st–4th avenues

Central Link Westlake

Good

HIGHLIGHTS

Top Things To Eat
● Smoked salmon pate pastry from Piroshky Piroshky
● Pike Place Chowder
● Sandwiches from Cycene
● Marionberry Pie Greek Yogurt from Ellenos
Top Shops
● Indi Chocolate
● Lamplight Books
● MarketSpice
● Tenzing Momo
● Ugly Baby and La Ru

TIP

● The rooftop garden at the market is a great quiet place to enjoy a picnic lunch with an ocean view.

Pioneer Square

Enjoy a blend of ancient and modern combined in Pioneer Square

THE BASICS

Pioneer Square
pioneersquare.org
⊞ E16
✉ Yesler Way to King Street and 2nd Avenue to Elliott Bay; visitor information booth in Occidental Square in summer
Klondike Gold Rush National Historical Park
nps.gov/klse/index.htm
✉ 319 2nd Avenue S
☎ 206/220-4240
🕐 Late May–early Sep daily 9–5; early Sep–late May 10–5
🚌 Lots of options to Pioneer Square Station
🚊 Central Link: Pioneer Square
💵 Free

HIGHLIGHTS

● The pergola at 1st and Yesler
● Smith Tower
● Occidental Park (▷ 34)
● Klondike Gold Rush National Historical Park
● Waterfall Garden Park

Constructed after the Great Seattle Fire, Pioneer Square's brick buildings retain an architectural integrity you won't find elsewhere in the city.

From the ashes In 1852, Seattle's pioneers moved across Elliott Bay and built the first permanent settlement in what is now Pioneer Square. The area burned to the ground in 1889, but was quickly rebuilt. When gold was discovered in the Yukon, prospectors converged on Pioneer Square to board ships to Alaska, and the area became the primary outfitting post for miners. Take Bill Speidel's Underground Tour (▷ 118) for further interesting and entertaining historical information.

Moving through the square Pioneer Square's most notable landmarks include Smith Tower (▷ 35), which has an observation deck, and the lovely glass-and-iron pergola at 1st and Yesler. Interesting stores line 1st Avenue south of Yesler. Walk through the lovely Grand Central Arcade, which opens onto Occidental Park (▷ 34), cross Main Street, and stop to visit the Klondike Gold Rush National Historical Park.

Detours Take a short detour to enchanting Waterfall Park at 2nd and South Main; then backtrack to the bricked pedestrian walkway, and amble along the cobblestoned Occidental Place, taking time to explore the cluster of art galleries that extend around the corner to 1st and South Jackson.

TOP 25

Seattle Aquarium and the Waterfront

Seafood shacks, quirky souvenir stalls, and some of Seattle's best attractions are all on the waterfront—a dynamic area with exciting plans for the future.

Seattle Aquarium This is the place to acquaint yourself with Pacific Northwest marine life. In the Underwater Dome room you can watch Puget Sound's "underworld" pass before your eyes as sharks, sturgeon and salmon swim by. The Window on Washington Waters features dive shows, and the replica tidal pools allow for a true hands-on experience where you can touch sea urchins, sea stars and hermit crabs. Meet the sea otters and harbor seals at their daily feedings, and catch a glimpse of the giant Pacific octopus in the Life of a Drifter exhibit.

Wings Over Washington This "flying theatre" will provide you with a different perspective of the waterfront. Once you are strapped into your seat it will transport you on an aerial adventure across the state of Washington, soaring over sea cliffs, mountains and valleys.

The Waterfront going forward From Native American winter village to the site of a steam-powered sawmill and an important trading port, Seattle's waterfront has been altered significantly over the last 150 years. Plans over the next decade are underway to renew the area from Belltown down to Pioneer Square, creating a new promenade, seawall, bike path and waterfront park, and to expand Pike Place Market.

THE BASICS

Aquarium
seattleaquarium.org
⊞ C15
⊠ Pier 59: 1483 Alaskan Way at Pike Street
☎ 206/386-4300
🕓 Jul–Aug daily 9.30–7; Sep–Jun 9.30–5
🍴 Aquarium Café
🚌 99
♿ Very good
✋ Expensive; reduction with CityPass

Waterfront
⊠ Alaskan Way between Broad (pier 70) and Main (pier 48)

Seattle Great Wheel
seattlegreatwheel.com
⊞ D15
⊠ 1301 Alaskan Way
☎ 206/623-8607

Wings over Washington
wingsoverwa.com
⊞ D15
⊠ 1301 Alaskan Way
☎ 206/602-1803

HIGHLIGHTS

Aquarium
● Children's touch tidal pools
● Underwater Dome room
Waterfront
● Bell Street complex restaurants and marina
● Seattle Great Wheel

DOWNTOWN TOP 25

Seattle Art Museum

HIGHLIGHTS

● Jonathan Borofsky's sculpture *Hammering Man*
● Indigenous art of Africa, Oceania and the Americas
● The Katherine White collection of African sculpture
● Pacific Northwest collection

TIP

● Admission is free on first Thursday of the month (special exhibits are also half price).

One of the city's best attractions is the Seattle Art Museum, featuring big names in the art world including Pollock, Rembrandt, and Monet. The antique global treasures are impressive, too.

Another world The steel-and-glass-fronted structure of the Seattle Art Museum (SAM), opened in 1991 and expanded in 2008, steps up the hill between 1st and 2nd avenues. To reach the galleries, you ascend a grand staircase, walking the gauntlet between monumental paired rams, guardian figures, and sacred camels from the Ming dynasty.

Dazzling collections SAM's permanent collections range from the indigenous art of Africa, Oceania and the Americas to modern US

The Hammering Man, Jonathan Borofsky, 1991 (left); Native American art, and further galleries with art from Oceania and Africa (top and bottom middle); Modern and Contemporary Galleries, with Importune: Stage 1 by Cai Guo-Qiang (right)

paintings and sculpture. Other galleries feature European exhibitions from the Medieval period through the 19th century. A Northwest Coast collection features large pieces, including four full-scale carved Kwakiutl houseposts. In other galleries, the museum presents traveling exhibitions and launches major shows of its own. Recent exhibitions have featured modernism in the Pacific Northwest, nature and pattern in Japanese design, and paintings and drawings of the European avant-garde.

Hammering Man Of the 48ft (15m) sculpture out front, sculptor Jonathan Borofsky has said: "I want this work to appeal to all people of Seattle—not just artists, but families young and old. At its heart, society reveres the worker. The *Hammering Man* is the worker in all of us."

THE BASICS

seattleartmuseum.org

✚ D15

✉ 1300 1st Avenue

☎ 206/654-3100

🕐 Wed–Sun 10–5 (Thu until 9). Closed some public holidays

🍽 Taste

🚌 10, 29, 41, 47, 71

🚇 Central Link: University Street

♿ Very good

💰 Expensive

Seattle Central Library

TOP 25

The Central Library is architecturally inspiring, both inside (left) and out (right)

THE BASICS

spl.org

➕ E15

✉ 1000 4th Avenue

☎ 206/386-4636

🕐 Mon–Thu 10–8,
Fri–Sat 10–6, Sun 12–6

🍴 FriendShop

🚌 2, 12, 21, 55, 56, 57

🚉 Central Link:
University Street

💵 Free

❓ Free self-guided cell-
phone tours are available.
Brochures with more information are available at the
welcome desks or online.

DID YOU KNOW?

● The design of the building has various sustain-
able and environmentally-
friendly features including
an irrigation system for the
exterior landscaping that's
fed by a 38,500-gallon
rainwater collection tank.

● Free special events
are hosted weekly at this
library branch, including
movie screenings, lectures
and discussions.

**Serving as a civic icon for the city, the
Seattle Public Library's Central Library is
an architectural marvel, inside and out,
that's both user-friendly and an inviting
public learning and gathering space.**

Architecture The 11-story concrete, glass and
steel building was designed and built in 2004
by Dutch Rem Koolhaas and Seattle native
Joshua Prince-Ramus. Resembling a series of
complicated geometric shapes stacked atop
of each other on the exterior, the light-filled
interior too is contemporary in its design with
angular walls, high ceilings, wide open view-
points, and bright pops of colour throughout.

What's inside Design meets function here
where over one-million books and other materi-
als are arranged on four open floors along the
Books Spiral, with a gently sloping ramp that
connects all four floors in one continuous walkway. Other levels include a Children's Center
that even has an area for stroller parking; a
Learning Center for ESL visitors that offers
classes and citizenship resources; and the
Mixing Chamber for general information and
research with help from the librarians.

Extras Throughout the library there is public art
on the walls, free WiFi, and 400 public computers to use. There's also a gift shop, and a café.
Head to the 10th floor for an amazing view of
the city and Elliott Bay or lounge in the Reading
Room and read under 40-foot high ceilings.

The Wing Luke Asian Museum

The museum's red-brick exterior (left); The Letter Cloud exhibit (right)

A piece of Seattle's historic Chinatown is preserved inside this modern museum, where visitors are offered a glimpse into the lives of early Asian-American pioneers that came to the city over a century ago.

The name A Smithsonian affiliated museum, the Wing Luke Museum of the Asian Pacific American Experience was founded in 1967 to honor the late Wing Chong Luke the first Asian-American official elected to public office in the Pacific Northwest. The Wing's collection now includes over 18,000 artifacts, photographs, documents and books.

The building The Wing is housed in the historic East Kong Yick Building from 1910. It's one of two red-brick buildings whose construction was funded by a group of Chinese immigrants. Inside, the original old growth lumber has been preserved and the exhibits on the first two floors tell stories about Asian immigrants that have shaped the Pacific Northwest from the early pioneer days to influencing current day issues and trends.

Preserved heritage On the top two floors, visited only via the guided tour which is included in the admission price, are a family association room featuring pressed tin ceilings and tables displaying vintage ivory mahjong tiles, and several modest apartments with a communal kitchen from 1942, which were part of the former Freeman Hotel.

THE BASICS

wingluke.org

➕ F17

✉ 719 S King Street

☎ 206/623-5124

🕐 Tue–Sun 10–5 (until 8 on 1st Thu of month)

🍴 No

🚌 1, 7, 14, 36, 29, 70, 99

🚉 Chinatown-International District

♿ Good

💲 Moderate

HIGHLIGHT

● The old general store, Yick Fung Co., which operated from 1910 until 2008, was one of the first Chinese stores in the city It is wonderfully preserved with antique woks, jars of dried fruit and medicine, woven baskets and tinned goods.

TIP

● Free monthly events are hosted at the museum, including film screenings, family fun days and lectures.

More to See

5TH AVENUE THEATRE
5thavenue.org
Built in 1926, this ornately carved theater is decorated in patterns after the imperial throne room in Beijing's Forbidden City. It regularly hosts productions of classic musicals and touring Broadway shows.
➕ E14 ✉ 1308 5th Avenue ☎ 206/625-1418 🚌 101 ❓ Tours: Mondays at 12, free but registration required.

1201 THIRD AVENUE
Locally nicknamed the "Spark Plug," this late 80s postmodern-style commercial building is the second tallest structure in Seattle and is an iconic part of the city skyline. The Brooklyn restaurant (▷ 42) at the base has some of the best oysters in town.
➕ E15 ✉ 1201 3rd Avenue

FRYE ART MUSEUM
fryemuseum.org
This beautiful, spacious gallery devoted to representational art rotates works from the permanent collection, most notably pieces by William Merritt Chase, Winslow Homer, John Singer Sargeant and Renoir. The museum also regularly hosts free concerts.
➕ F15 ✉ 704 Terry Avenue ☎ 206/622-9250 🕐 Tue–Sun 11–5 (Thu until 7) 🍴 Café Frieda 🚌 3, 4, 12, 60 ⓔ Excellent 🆓 Free ❓ Sun afternoon concerts, films, workshops and lectures

MYRTLE EDWARDS PARK
With a winding 1.25-mile (2-km) pedestrian and bicycle path along the shore of Elliott Bay, this urban park has some of the best views in the city of the Olympic Mountains, Mount Rainier and Puget Sound. It is great for birdwatching and has the Olympic Sculpture Park (▷ 26) at its southern end.
➕ A13 ✉ 3130 Alaskan Way 🚌 33

OCCIDENTAL PARK
Also referred to as Occidental Square and Occidental Mall, this former parking lot is a welcoming public space in the Pioneer Square

Inside the beautiful 5th Avenue Theatre

district surrounded by art galleries, food trucks and leafy trees. The totem poles and woodcarvings are by American artist Duane Pasco. The bronze Fallen Firefighters Memorial is by Chinese American sculptor Hai Ying Wu.

➕ E16 ✉ Occidental Avenue S and S Main in Pioneer Square 🚌 99

SMITH TOWER

smithtower.com

When it opened in 1914, Smith Tower was Seattle's first steel-framed skyscraper and the tallest building outside of New York City. At 38 stories, it remained the tallest building west of the Mississippi until 1962. For a fee, you can ride to the 35th floor in the company of the last of Seattle's elevator attendants to get a sweeping view of Downtown and gain access to the bar.

➕ E16 ✉ 506 2nd Avenue and Yesler Way ☎ 206/624-0414 🕐 Observation deck Sun–Wed 10–10, Thu–Sat 10–11 💲 Inexpensive (tickets for after 6pm are discounted)

WASHINGTON STATE CONVENTION CENTER

wscc.com

On Level 2 of the Convention Center, the Rotating Art Gallery features over 100 works of fine art on display for the public to view for free. Often there are special traveling exhibits here as well.

➕ E14 ✉ 705 Pike Street ☎ 206/694-5000 🕐 Daily 7am–10pm 🚇 Central Link: Westlake

WESTLAKE PARK

With its potted plants, fountain and colorful furniture, this pleasant little plaza in the heart of Downtown is a good place to take a break from shopping, enjoy an outdoor concert or movie, play ping-pong or get lunch from the food trucks. It has a holiday carousel and pop-up market in the winter, and is part of the Urban Parks Art programme showcasing the work of urban artists.

➕ D14 ✉ Along Pine St and 4th Ave 🚇 Monorail from Seattle Center; Central Link to Westlake Station.

Family beachcombing at Myrtle Edwards Park

Smith Tower, one of the buildings in Pioneer Square

Downtown Stroll

Dive into the city's hectic center, visiting the famed Pike Place Market, the Waterfront, Pioneer Square and the entertaining retail core.

DISTANCE: 2.8 miles (4km) **ALLOW:** 1.5 hours

START

PIKE STREET AT 8TH AVENUE
✚ E14 🚌 7, 10, 11, 43, 47, 49, 63, 64
🚉 Central Link: Westlake

END

FAIRMONT OLYMPIC HOTEL
✚ E15 🚌 19, 24, 33, 37, 57, 64
🚉 Central Link: University Street

❶ Begin your walk from the Washington State Convention Center (▷ 35) at Pike Street and 8th Avenue. Walk west along Pike Street to 5th Avenue.

❽ Walk north on 5th Avenue to the Fairmont Olympic Hotel (▷ 112) and have a celebratory cocktail in the elegant Terrace Lounge.

❷ Turn left, and walk towards University Street, stopping briefly to peek inside the ornate 5th Avenue Theatre (▷ 34).

❼ Walk south along either Western Avenue or Alaskan Way (on the Waterfront) to Yesler Way. Go left and head east into Pioneer Square (▷ 28). Be sure to see Occidental Park (▷ 34), a leafy, brick-lined pedestrian plaza.

❸ Head west along University Street, turning right on 4th Avenue. Continue north two blocks until Westlake Park between Pike Street and Pine Street.

❻ Walk east to 1st Avenue and then south to University, where the Seattle Art Museum (▷ 30–31) welcomes visitors. Cross the street and descend the Harbor Steps.

❹ Take in the live music and buskers that make this one of Seattle's most lively locations. Walk west on Pine Street until you hit Pike Place and stop to browse the stalls in its legendary market (▷ 27).

❺ Take some time to cruise through the stalls and shops; if hunger strikes, opportunities for snacking abound.

Shopping

AGATE DESIGNS

agatedesigns.com

This neat little museum-like shop is filled with crystals, gemstones, fossils carvings and jewelry.

➕ E16 ✉ 120 1st Avenue S ☎ 206/621-3063 ⏰ Mon–Sat 10–6, Sun 11–4

ALHAMBRA

alhambrastyle.com

Luxury boutique for women featuring fine organic cottons, silks and velvets from global designers. On Saturdays a live jazz band adds to the atmosphere.

➕ D14 ✉ 2127 1st Avenue ☎ 206/621-9571 ⏰ Mon–Sat 10–6.30, Sun 12–5

AZUMA GALLERY

azumagallery.com

An established art gallery showcasing traditional and modern Japanese works including screen prints, paintings, ceramics and craftwork.

➕ E17 ✉ 530 1st Avenue S ☎ 206/622-5599 ⏰ Tue–Sat 12.30–5.30

BABY & COMPANY

babyandco.us

A Seattle-based, high-end fashion fixture since the 70s, this women's and men's clothing store specializes in contemporary designer pieces.

➕ D14 ✉ 1936 1st Avenue ☎ 206/448-4077 ⏰ Mon–Sat 10–6, Sun 12–5

THE BELFRY

thebelfryoddities.com

Seattle is full of odd and quirky shops, and this one nearly tops the list. From the mysterious to the macabre, The Belfry sells vintage taxidermy, bones of all sorts, framed natural history specimens, and other things curios.

➕ E16 ✉ 309A Third Avenue S ☎ 206/682-2951 ⏰ Mon–Fri 10–6, Sat 11–5

DAISO

daisojapan.com

Located inside the Westlake Center shopping mall, this is Japan's version of a dollar store only better. Wander the isles of imported Japanese sweets, toiletries, ceramics, stationery, toys and accessories. There are several locations in the city, including one in Chinatown.

➕ D14 ✉ 400 Pine Street ☎ 206/447-6211 ⏰ Mon–Sat 10–8, Sun 11–6

EIGHTH GENERATION

eighthgeneration.com

Native American-owned and operated souvenir shop that sells authentic, contemporary Native American wool blankets, jewelry and prints.

➕ D15 ✉ 93 Pike Street ☎ 206/430-6233 ⏰ Daily 10–5

FACERE JEWELRY ART GALLERY

facerejewelryart.com

Presenting the works of over 50 jewelry artists from all over the world, as well as antique and vintage pieces, this is the place for finding that one-of-a-kind item.

➕ E14 ✉ 1420 5th Avenue ☎ 206/624-6768 ⏰ Mon–Sat 10–6

FILSON

filson.com

Established in Seattle in 1897, this outdoor clothing company started off making gear for the Klondike Gold Rush prospectors. They still make items locally, such as luggage and leather wallets.

➕ Off map ✉ 1741 1st Avenue S ☎ 206/622-3147 ⏰ Mon–Sat 10–6, Sun 12–5

FLURY & CO. GALLERY

fluryco.com

This is one of the leading galleries dealing with works by American

photographer and ethnologist Edward S. Curtis (1868–1952). His sepia-toned portraits and notes provide an invaluable record of Native American history.
➕ E16 ✉ 322 1st Avenue S ☎ 206/587-0260 🕐 Mon–Sat 11–6

FOX'S
foxsseattle.com
This century-old Seattle jeweler features exquisite contemporary, classic and vintage diamond rings and other finery.
➕ E15 ✉ 405 University Street ☎ 206/623-2528 🕐 Tue–Sat 10–6

GLASSHOUSE STUDIO
glasshouse-studio.com
The Northwest's oldest glass-blowing studio produces beautiful pieces, sold—along with the work of 40 other artists.
➕ E17 ✉ 311 Occidental Avenue S ☎ 206/682-9939 🕐 Mon–Sat 10–5, Sun 11–4; glass-blowing demonstrations Mon–Sat 10–11.30 and 1–5

GREG KUCERA GALLERY
gregkucera.com
Spacious, contemporary art gallery representing top Northwest artists, including sculpture on an outdoor deck.
➕ E16 ✉ 212 3rd Avenue S ☎ 206/624-0770 🕐 Tue–Sat 10.30–5.30, Sun 1–5

KUHLMAN
kuhlmanseattle.com
For the perfect bespoke suit, this boutique sells fine shirts, jackets and pants, women's clothing, ties and watches.
➕ C13 ✉ 2419 1st Avenue ☎ 206/441-1999 🕐 Mon–Sat 11–7, Sun 12–6

THE LONDON PLANE
thelondonplaneseattle.com
Part grocery store, part café, this elegant concept space sells housewares,

hostess gifts, wine and flowers. Visit just for the fresh baked breads and pastries.
➕ E16 ✉ 300 Occidental Avenue S ☎ 206/624-1374 🕐 Mon–Tue 8–5, Wed–Fri 8–9, Sat 9–9, Sun 9–3

MADE IN WASHINGTON
madeinwashington.com
Souvenir store that specializes in items made in the region, such as gourmet foods, handcrafted art, chocolate, bath and body products, and gifts for pets.
➕ D14 ✉ 1530 Post Alley ☎ 206/467-0788 🕐 Daily 10–6

MAGIC MOUSE TOYS
magicmousetoys.com
Classic Seattle shop with two floors stuffed with quality toys, puzzles, books, costumes, and games for all ages.
➕ E16 ✉ 603 1st Avenue ☎ 206/682-8097 🕐 Daily 10–6

MARIO'S
marios.mitchellstores.com
Beautiful designer boutique for men and women's clothing, shoes, and accessories from the top names of the fashion industry.
➕ E14 ✉ 1513 6th Avenue ☎ 206/223-1461 🕐 Mon–Sat 10–6, Sun 12–5

MARKET MAGIC SHOP
marketmagicshop.com
One of Pike Place Market's most entertaining shops, this is where professional magicians replenish their supplies, and

GALLERY WALKS
On the first Thursday of the month, Pioneer Square galleries and those in the Pike Place Market area open into the evening for the monthly art walk. Many galleries take this opportunity to preview their new shows.

where budding houdinis get their start. Staff perform tricks for eager onlookers, while other patrons wait to have their fortunes told.

🔲 D14 ✉ 1st level below the food stalls, Pike Place Market ☎ 206/624-4271 🕐 Sun–Fri 10–5.30, Sat 9.30–6

MOMO

momoseattle.com

Japanese accessories, greeting cards, home accents and clothing for all ages that are whimsical and hard to find elsewhere. While some items are straight imports from Japan, other products are from Hawaii and the Pacific Northwest.

🔲 F17 ✉ 600 S Jackson Street ☎ 206/329-4736 🕐 Mon–Sat 11–6, Sun 12–5

MOOREA SEAL

mooreaseal.com

Gorgeous jewelry, handmade stationery, recycled clothing, and giftable housewares—7 percent of all proceeds go towards non-profitable organizations.

🔲 D15 ✉ 1012 1st Avenue ☎ 206/728-2523 🕐 Daily 10–7

NORDSTROM

nordstrom.com

A Seattle original dating back to 1901, this luxury department store stocks clothing and shoes, accessories, cosmetics and home decor.

🔲 E14 ✉ 500 Pine Street ☎ 206/628-2111 🕐 Mon–Fri 9.30–9, Sat 10–9, Sun 10.30–7

PETER MILLER BOOKS

petermiller.com

A fitting match to the building it's located in, this polished bookstore sells mostly titles in architecture and design, plus some stationery and housewares.

🔲 E16 ✉ 304 Alaskan Way S ☎ 206/441-1501 🕐 Mon–Sat 10–6

SEATTLE ANTIQUES MARKET

seattleantiquesmarket.com

Browse through vintage magazines, lost photographs, antique furniture, old toys and loads more at this store by the aquarium. There's free car parking but obey the signage or risk being towed.

🔲 D15 ✉ 1400 Alaskan Way ☎ 206/623-6115 🕐 Daily 10–6

SOIL GALLERY

soilart.org

An artist-run non-profit space with excellent, often boundary-pushing exhibits by emerging local talent in various media.

🔲 E16 ✉ 112 3rd Avenue S ☎ 206/264-8061 🕐 Thu–Sun 12–5

STEINBRUECK NATIVE GALLERY

steinbruecknativegallery.com

Ceremonial masks, drums, boxes, prints, baskets, and other craft art by local Native Americans adorn the walls of this gallery. The Inuit pieces from the Arctic and Alaska are beautiful too, ma from serpentine, bone and ivory.

🔲 C14 ✉ 2030 Western Avenue B ☎ 206/441-3821 🕐 Mon–Sat 10–5, Sun 11–5

TRAVER GALLERY

travergallery.com

Contemporary painting, sculpture, ceramics and glass by major artists, including works by Dale Chihuly.

🔲 D15 ✉ 110 Union, 2nd floor ☎ 206/587-6501 🕐 Tue–Fri 10–6, Sat 10–5, Sun 12–5

WORLD SPICE MERCHANTS

worldspice.com

It's worth coming here just for the aroma, but the huge selection of spices, and teas are not to be sniffed at.

🔲 D15 ✉ 1509 Western Avenue, by Pike Place Market ☎ 206/682-7274 🕐 Mon–Sat 10–6, Sun 11–6

Entertainment and Nightlife

ACT—A CONTEMPORARY THEATRE

acttheatre.org

A wide-ranging and full program in the five theaters here includes drama, musicals, dance, comedy and cabaret.

➕ E14 ✉ 700 Union Street ☎ 206/292-7660; box office 206/292-7676

BATHTUB GIN & CO

bathtubginseattle.com

Tucked away in a former boiler room in the basement of an old brick apartment building, this little speakeasy bar serves up great cocktails in a warm atmosphere.

➕ C14 ✉ 2205 2nd Avenue ☎ 206/728-6069

BLACK BOTTLE

blackbottleseattle.com

This self-described "gastro-tavern" serves gourmet dishes at reasonable prices. Later in the evening, it turns into one of Belltown's liveliest spots.

➕ C13 ✉ 2600 1st Avenue ☎ 206/441-1500

BRANCHWATER

branchwaterseattle.com

Kentucky Bourbon whiskey bar in the heart of Belltown, ideal for cooler, rainy days with its warm and dark wooden interior. The little patio outside has a cozy fire pit and a snack menu.

➕ C13 ✉ 2219 4th Avenue ☎ 206/441-4777

THE CROCODILE

thecrocodile.com

Local and national touring bands play here at this birthplace of grunge where Nirvana, Pearl Jam, Alice in Chains, and many others have performed.

➕ C13 ✉ 2200 2nd Avenue ☎ 206/441-4618

DIMITRIOU'S JAZZ ALLEY

jazzalley.com

Well-known intimate jazz club with a lovely dinner menu. First-class acts have played here since the late 70s. And as a nice bonus, the parking is free.

➕ D13 ✉ 2033 6th Avenue ☎ 206/441-9729

FENIX

fenixunderground.com

A new "Fenix" rose from the rubble after earthquake damage destroyed the club. Live music, from rock to world music.

➕ E16 ✉ 101 S Washington Street ☎ 206/405-4323

FIRESIDE ROOM

hotelsorrento.com

With its overstuffed chairs and fireplace, this spot in the stately Hotel Sorrento takes you back to earlier, more genteel times. Occasionally live music is performed here as well.

➕ F15 ✉ 900 Madison Street ☎ 206/622-6400

HIGHWAY 99 BLUES CLUB

highway99blues.com

Top-class blues acts play in an intimate setting with a great old-timey atmosphere. Get there early for a good seat—lots of pillars block sightlines from some areas. Good Southern food too.

➕ D15 ✉ 1414 Alaskan Way, across from the aquarium ☎ 206/382-2171

HAPPY HOUR

Look out for signs in the windows of bars and restaurants, as between the hours of 4pm and 6pm (this varies), many places offer a Happy Hour menu on their drinks and food. This means discounted prices, sometimes by as much as half price.

THE PARAMOUNT THEATRE

paramount.com

Seattle's premiere main-stage for the concert tours of superstars and for traveling musical theater productions. Built in 1928 as a silent film and vaudeville house, it has been beautifully restored.

E13 ⊠ 911 Pine Street ☎ 205/682-1414

THE PIKE PUB & BREWERY

pikebrewing.com

Popular for its good food, excellent craft beers and affordable prices. Tours of the brewery are available for a fee but their Microbrewery Museum is free.

D15 ⊠ 1415 1st Avenue (in the Market) ☎ 206/622- 6044

QUEEN CITY GRILL

qcgrestaurant.com

Classy and lively Belltown bar and restaurant from 1910 with an excellent wine list, bar menu and outdoor patio.

C14 ⊠ 2201 1st Avenue ☎ 206/441-4311

RADIATOR WHISKEY

radiatorwhiskey.com

Enormous whiskey list, easy atmosphere, and some popular but conversation-starting menu items such as Fried Beef Lip Terrine and Smoked Half Pig Head.

D14 ⊠ 94 Pike Street (in Pike Place Market) ☎ 206/457-4268

SAFECO FIELD

seattlemariners.com

The Seattle Mariners play at this state-of-the-art ballpark. The open-air stadium seats 47,000 and has a retractable roof. Baseball season runs from spring into fall; tours are available year-round.

Off map ⊠ 1250 1st Avenue S at Royal Brougham ☎ 206/346-4001 for tickets

TAVOLÀTA

ethanstowellrestaurants.com

This industrial yet homey restaurant and bar serves an incredible menu of Italian classics, but it's also one of the most visually stunning bars in Belltown. A place to see and be seen.

C13 ⊠ 2323 2nd Avenue ☎ 206/838-8008

THEATERSPORTS

unexpectedproductions.org

Two teams battle it out in a comedy improv show at the Market Theater that's scored by a panel of judges. Audience suggestions are welcomed and the best ones can win a prize.

E15 ⊠ 1428 Post Alley at the Pike Street Market ☎ 206/587-2414 🕐 Fri, Sat at 10pm, Sun at 7pm

VON'S 1000 SPIRITS

vons1000spirits.com

Family-friendly gastropub with a huge selection of drinks, good comfort food, and a great Happy Hour menu.

E14 ⊠ 1225 1st Avenue ☎ 206/621-8667

OUTDOOR CONCERTS

In summer, Seattleites enjoy several outdoor concert series, including:

● Free Out-to-Lunch noontime concerts at various Downtown locations.

● BECU ZooTunes, a summer-long outdoor concert series at the Woodland Park Zoo.

● Free Concerts at the Mural in August at the Seattle Center.

● Ballard SeafoodFest, a free festival featuring numerous alternative rock bands.

● Capitol Hill Block Party, with three days of live music and entertainment.

● West Seattle Summerfest, a free family-friendly event with music and beer gardens.

Where to Eat

THE BROOKLYN SEAFOOD, STEAK & OYSTER BAR ($$$)

thebrooklyn.com

Fresh, local oysters are the specialty here, but any of the other dishes are excellent, too. Happy Hour is 4–6pm.

🞥 E15 ✉ 1212 2nd Avenue ☎ 206/224-7000 🕐 Lunch Mon–Fri, dinner nightly

CAFÉ CAMPAGNE ($$)

cafecampagne.com

This cozy spot in the Pike Place Market is perfect for a glass of wine. Sunday brunch is one of the best.

🞥 D14 ✉ 1600 Post Alley ☎ 206/728-2233 🕐 Lunch and dinner daily, weekend brunch

CHAN ($$)

chanseattle.com

Modern Korean gastropub with tradtional favorites such as *bibimbap*, *bulgogi*, seafood pancakes and *kimchi*.

🞥 D14 ✉ 86 Pine Street ☎ 206/443-5443 🕐 Dinner Tue–Sat

COPAL ($$)

copalseattle.com

Feast on tacos and tropical cocktails in an airy space with a wood-fired stove.

🞥 E17 ✉ 323 Occidental Avenue S ☎ 206/682-1117 🕐 Dinner Mon–Sat, lunch Mon–Fri

THE CRAB POT ($$$)

thecrabpotseattle.com

The waterfront location and come-as-you-are appeal is perfect for families. Don a bib and crack your crab right on the paper-lined tables.

🞥 D15 ✉ 1301 Alaskan Way (pier 57) ☎ 206/624-1890 🕐 Lunch and dinner daily

DAHLIA BAKERY ($)

dahliabakery.com

The artisan breads, pastries, and other cakes are pretty super, as are the breakfast sandwiches.

🞥 D14 ✉ 2001 4th Avenue ☎ 206/441-4540 🕐 Breakfast and lunch daily

DAHLIA LOUNGE ($$$)

dahlialounge.com

Top Seattle Chef Tom Douglas' original restaurant with true farm-to-table fare. The menu features Pacific Northwest cuisine with an Asian twist. Try their famous Triple Coconut Cream Pie.

🞥 D14 ✉ 2001 4th Avenue ☎ 206/682-4142 🕐 Lunch Mon–Fri, dinner nightly

EGGS AND PLANTS ($)

eggsandplants.com

For vegetarians and non-vegetarians alike, this Mediterranean joint makes exceptional sandwiches with fluffy pita bread, stuffed with hummus and other vegetarian goodies. The view into the glass-blowing studio is an added bonus.

🞥 C13 ✉ 2229 5th Avenue ☎ 206/448-2050 🕐 Daily 10–8

ELM COFFEE ROASTERS ($)

elmcoffeeroasters.com

Spacious, bright, and modern coffee shop where the well-sourced, single-origin beans are roasted on site at the back. Their delicious fresh pastries come from The London Plane bakery a few blocks away. Try the house-made hazelnut milk, too.

🞥 E16 ✉ 240 2nd Avenue S ☎ 206/445-7808 🕐 Mon–Fri 7–6, Sat 8–6, Sun 9–5

FARESTART ($$)

farestart.org

This non-profit restaurant serves delicious, hearty meals at budget prices while training homeless men and women for jobs in the food service industry. The weekday lunch buffet is popular, and on Thursday nights top chefs from local restaurants prepare outstanding dinners. All proceeds go back into the program.

➕ D14 ✉ 700 Virginia Street ☎ 206/267-7601 🕐 Lunch Mon–Fri, dinner Thu only

FOB POKE BAR ($)

fobpokebar.com

Take out or eat in customizable Hawaiian poke bowls that are filled with fresh, raw and seasoned fish, rice, vegetables and savoury toppings.

➕ C13 ✉ 220 Blanchard Street ☎ 206/728-9888 🕐 Lunch and dinner daily

IL CORVO ($)

ilcorvopasta.com

Possibly the best pasta in the state, this little Italian hotspot has line-ups out the door during lunch time. Fresh, organically made pasta dishes are offered and most are just $10.

➕ E16 ✉ 217 James Street ☎ 206/538-0099 🕐 Lunch only, Mon–Fri

IVAR'S ($$)

ivars.com

Ask anyone for fish and chips in Seattle and they'll send you to Ivar's. The casual fish bars are ideal for an easy lunch.

➕ D15 ✉ 1001 Alaskan Way (Pier 54) ☎ 206/624-6852 🕐 Lunch and dinner daily

JACK'S FISH SPOT ($)

jacksfishspot.com

Fun, fast, and fresh seafood from this busy market stall. Try their *cioppino*, the fish-and-chips with garlic fries, or the crab cocktail.

➕ D14 ✉ 1514 Pike Place Market ☎ 206/467-0514 🕐 Lunch daily

LOULAY $$$

thechefinthehat.com

Chef Thierry Rautureau uses the freshest local ingredients for his very French menus in this classy restaurant.

➕ E14 ✉ 600 Union Street ☎ 206/402-4588 🕐 Breakfast, lunch and dinner daily

MACRINA BAKERY ($)

macrinabakery.com

Fresh breads and pastries, and shots of espresso greet sleepy urbanites.

➕ C14 ✉ 2408 1st Avenue ☎ 206/448-4032 🕐 Daily 7am–6pm

MANEKI ($$)

manekirestaurant.com

An International District standby, founded in 1923. Stellar sushi only made better by outstanding service.

➕ F16 ✉ 304 6th Avenue S ☎ 206/622-2631 🕐 Dinner Tue–Sun

MATT'S IN THE MARKET ($$$)

mattsinthemarket.com

With views over Pike Place Market and Elliott Bay, this lively bistro is known for its seafood and service. Try the Pan-fried Cornmeal Crusted Catfish sandwich.

➕ D14 ✉ 94 Pike Street, Suite 32 ☎ 206/467-7909 🕐 Lunch and dinner Mon–Sat

THE METROPOLITAN GRILL ($$$)

themetropolitangrill.com

Stellar steaks and legendary martinis draw crowds. Happy Hour features inexpensive food specials in the bar.

➕ E16 ✉ 820 2nd Avenue ☎ 206/624-3287 🕐 Lunch Mon–Fri, dinner nightly

PALACE KITCHEN ($$)

palacekitchen.com

Probably one of Chef Tom Douglas' best restaurants, with a rich American menu.

🏥 D13 ✉ 2030 5th Avenue ☎ 206/448-2001 🕐 Dinner daily until 1am

PANAMA HOTEL TEA & COFFEE HOUSE ($)

panamahotel.net

This International District café serves up more than 20 varieties of tea in a building that was once a Japanese bathhouse.

🏥 F16 ✉ 605 S Main Street ☎ 206/515-4000 🕐 Mon–Sat 10–9, Sun 9–9

LE PICHET ($$)

lepichetseattle.com

Café au lait in the morning, baguettes at lunch, and *charcuterie* and ever-changing specials at night make for casual French café dining at its best.

🏥 D14 ✉ 1933 1st Avenue ☎ 206/256-1499 🕐 Breakfast, lunch and dinner daily

PIKE PLACE CHOWDER ($)

pikeplacechowder.com

Award-winning chowder, and it comes in eight varieties including vegan. Order ahead of time online to skip the line-up.

🏥 D14 ✉ 1530 Post Alley ☎ 206/267-2537 🕐 Lunch and dinner daily

PINK DOOR ($$)

thepinkdoor.net

Located in Post Alley, this intimate Italian bistro has an outdoor deck with great views of Elliott Bay.

🏥 D14 ✉ 1919 Post Alley ☎ 206/443-3241 🕐 Lunch Mon–Sat, and dinner daily

SALUMI ($)

salumicuredmeats.com

Seattleites flock to this little lunch spot for great cured meat that has been cured onsite—for your own kitchen or in sandwiches. Come early or call ahead.

🏥 E16 ✉ 309 3rd Avenue S ☎ 206/621-8772 🕐 Lunch Mon–Fri

SERIOUS PIE ($$)

seriouspieseattle.com

Fantastic, gourmet, Neapolitan-style pizzas served in a warm, jovial atmosphere.

🏥 D14 ✉ 316 Virginia Street ☎ 206/838-7388 🕐 Lunch and dinner daily

SUSHI KASHIBA ($$$)

sushikashiba.com

This is top sushi Chef Shiro Kashiba's place, and sitting at the sushi bar is a must here. Order the *Omakase* (Chef's menu) for a great dining experience.

🏥 D14 ✉ 86 Pine Street ☎ 206/441-8844 🕐 Dinner daily

TAMARIND TREE ($$)

tamarindtreerestaurant.com

A standout Vietnamese restaurant in the heart of Little Saigon, with a romantic atmosphere and authentic menu.

🏥 G16 ✉ 1036 S Jackson Street, Suite A ☎ 206/860-1404 🕐 Lunch and dinner daily

TAYLOR SHELLFISH FARMS OYSTER BAR ($$)

taylorshellfishfarms.com

You'll find more than just oysters at this bar, where all the shellfish comes from their own Puget Sound fishery.

🏥 E16 ✉ 410 Occidental Avenue S ☎ 206/501-4060 🕐 Lunch and dinner daily

ZEITGEIST KUNST AND KAFFEE ($)

zeitgeistcoffee.com

Excellent espresso, local art on the exposed-brick walls, and lovely light lunch options.

🏥 E17 ✉ 171 S Jackson Street ☎ 206/583-0497 🕐 Mon–Fri 6–7, Sat 7–7, Sun 8–6

These two distinct neighborhoods are directly north of Downtown. Seattle Center, a 74-acre (30ha) city-owned civic park, is home to performance venues and museums, while Queen Anne Hill is a leafy residential paradise with prodigious views of the city, mountains and Puget Sound.

Highland   Drive

Prospect   Street

Ward   Street
Ward
Place

Aloha   Street

Valley   Street

Roy   Street

AURORA   AVENUE   NORTH

Avenue   North

Dexter   Street

Lake Union

MERCER   STREET

AURORA   AVENUE   NORTH

Harrison   Street

Avenue   North

Avenue   North

Thomas   Street

Dexter

8th

9TH   AVENUE   NORTH

John   Street

John   Street

Denny Park

DENNY   WAY

Alaskan Way Viaduct Replacement Tunnel under construction due to open 2019

John   Avenue   North

9th   Avenue

Taylor   Avenue   North

WALL   STREET

BATTERY   STREET

7th   Street

Bell   Avenue   Street

8th   Avenue

Blanchard   Street

**Monorail to
Seattle Center**

5th   Avenue

6TH   AVENUE

4TH AVENUE

C

D

Chihuly Garden and Glass

Glass appears to be growing at the Chihuly gallery (left), in the shadow of the Space Needle (right)

THE BASICS

chihulygardenand
glass.com

⊞ B12

✉ 305 Harrison Street at Seattle Center

☎ 206/753-4940

🕐 Open daily, hours vary so call ahead.

🍴 Collections Café

🚌 3, 4

🚈 Monorail

✋ Expensive

HIGHLIGHTS

● The Glasshouse
● *The Sun*
● *Glass Forest*
● *Persian Ceiling*

TIPS

● Time your visit so you can witness how the changing light transforms the outdoor exhibits as day turns into night.
● Children are allowed, but for peace of mind, you might want to leave them (and any clumsy adults) at home.

Tacoma-born Dale Chihuly is a world-renowned glass artist, and this extensive collection of his intricate and gloriously colorful works is displayed in a 1.5-acre (0.6ha) garden, a sparkling glasshouse and an eight-room exhibition hall.

The artist At the forefront of the development of glass as fine art, Dale Chihuly has examples of his work in many museums and public buildings around the world. After studying at the Rhode Island School of Design, he worked at Venice's Venini glass factory. Back in his home state, he co-founded the Pilchuck Glass School, near Seattle, and has been showered with awards for his art.

Garden and Glasshouse Some say you can't improve on nature, but this garden presents a compelling challenge to that belief, with colorful glass forms growing among the trees and flowers. The whole set piece is anchored by four stunning glass sculptures. The focal point is the Glasshouse, an arched structure housing a 100ft- (33m) long floral sculpture of richly glowing reds, oranges and yellows.

Exhibition and theater Eight galleries make up the exhibition, which displays some of Chihuly's finest works and traces the development of his ideas and techniques. The darkened rooms show the artworks to their best advantage, their vibrant colors and organic shapes gleaming through the gloom.

The distinctive form of the Museum of Pop Culture (left) holds a range of interesting exhibits (right)

TOP
25

This futuristic gathering place is half rock museum and half science fiction shrine—a temple to American music and science fiction unrivaled in both style and daring.

Gift to the city Microsoft co-founder Paul Allen idolized Seattle-born Jimi Hendrix and imagined a space to exhibit his personal collection of Hendrix memorabilia. Over time, the vision expanded beyond Hendrix: The museum would grow to explore all of American popular music, science fiction, and pop culture through a collection of engaging interactive and interpretive exhibits.

The design Allen hired renowned architect Frank O. Gehry to create a structure that was as rebellious and free-spirited as rock 'n' roll itself. To jumpstart his creative thinking, Gehry cut up and rearranged several electric guitars. This process gave birth to the museum's bold colors, swooping curves and reflective metal surface.

Discover what's inside The 85ft (26m) Sky Church features music, film and video by day and live bands by night. Trace the development of the electric guitar or view objects of Seattle's grunge scene, jam on real instruments in the Sound Lab, or record your own voice. The Science Fiction Museum pays tribute to the biggest names of the genre by displaying movie props, first editions and interviews with sci-fi pioneers. Other exhibits feature installations on horror films, video games and fantasy artwork.

THE BASICS

mopop.org

✚ C12

✉ 325 5th Avenue N at Seattle Center

☎ 206/770-2700 or 877/367-7361

🕐 Late May–Aug daily 10–7; Sep–late May 10–5

🚌 3, 4

🚡 Monorail

♿ Good

💲 Expensive

DID YOU KNOW?

● Jazz musician Les Paul pioneered electric guitar technology in Seattle by using a solid body. The Gibson company adopted the design and use it to this day.

● Jimi Hendrix was born in Seattle in 1942. In the late 1960s he revolutionized electric guitar playing with his radical fusion of jazz, rock, soul and blues.

TIP

Purchase your tickets online for a $2 discount.

Pacific Science Center

As you approach the Pacific Science Center, you enter another world. Gothic arches and an inner courtyard of pools, platforms and footbridges indicate you are in for something special.

Sputnik's legacy In 1962, the American scientific community was still smarting from the Soviet Union's unexpected launch of the Sputnik spacecraft. Determined to restore confidence in American science and technology, US officials pulled out all the stops when they built the US Science Pavilion for the Seattle World's Fair. The building reopened after the fair ended as the Pacific Science Center.

Science made easy A visit here can happily fill half a day. The exhibits bring scientific principles

The high arches of the Pacific Science Center (left); exploring the universe in the center's planetarium (below); children enjoying some of the many hands-on science exhibits (bottom left and right)

to life and make learning fun. In an outdoor exhibit, Water Works, you can use a water cannon to activate whirligigs or attempt to move a 2-ton ball suspended on water. Children can ride a high-rail bike for a bird's-eye view.

Hands on The Body Works exhibition lets you measure your stress level or grip strength or see what your face looks like with two left sides. Adventures in 3Dimensions shows how our brains process 3D imagery, and there are lots of robots—giant insects, dinosaurs and more—many of them interactive. Live animal exhibits include Insect Village and a Tropical Butterfly House. The Studio and the Portal to Current Research have regularly updated exhibits about new scientific and medical research. There's also a Planetarium and a live science stage.

THE BASICS

pacificsciencecenter.org

✚ B12

✉ 200 2nd Avenue N (Seattle Center)

☎ 206/443-2001, 206/443-2844

🕐 Mon–Fri 10–5, Sat–Sun 10–6

🍴 Fountains Café

🚌 1, 2 3, 4, 6, 8, 13, 15, 17, 18, 24, 33

🚝 Monorail

♿ Very good

✋ Expensive; half-price with CityPass

Space Needle

Almost everywhere you go in Seattle the Space Needle is there, towering over the city

THE BASICS

spaceneedle.com

➕ C12

✉ 400 Broad Street at Seattle Center

◉ Observation Deck daily 10–8

🍴 SkyCity Restaurant

🚌 3, 4

🚝 Monorail

♿ Wheelchair access

💲 Expensive; half-price with CityPass; free with dinner at restaurant

DID YOU KNOW?

● The Space Needle sways about 1in (3cm) for every 10mph (16kph) of wind.

● The Needle experienced an earthquake of 6.8 on the Richter scale (in 2001), and is equipped to withstand jolts up to 9.2.

The Space Needle's height and futuristic design have made it Seattle's most well-known landmark. From the observation deck, the view is stunning on a clear day.

The city's symbol The 605ft (184m) Space Needle was built in 1962 for Seattle's futuristic World's Fair. Rising 200ft (61m) above Seattle's highest hill, the structure is visible over a wide area. The steel structure weighs 3,700 tons and is anchored into the foundations with 72 huge bolts, each 32ft (10m) long by 4in (10cm) in diameter. The structure is designed to withstand winds up to 200mph (320kph). If you ride in the glass-walled elevator to the top during a snowstorm, it appears to be snowing upward.

Observation deck Each year, more than a million visitors ride one of the three glass elevators to the observation deck at the 520ft (159m) level. Newly renovated, the deck has floor-to-ceiling windows and information displays about what you can see. There are also screens linked to the rooftop. A reservation at the SkyCity Restaurant (▷ 56), at the 500ft (152m) level, gets you to the observation deck for free The restaurant rotates once every 47 minutes, giving a 360-degree view during your meal.

Tall and strong There are 848 steps between the bottom of the basement and the top of the Observation Deck. When the Space Needle was built in 1962, it was the tallest building west of the Mississippi River.

More to See

BILL & MELINDA GATES FOUNDATION DISCOVERY CENTER

gatesfoundation.org

Distributing grants in excess of $40 billion since 2000, the center has an inspiring visitor center.

🔶 C11 ✉ 440 5th Avenue N ☎ 206/709-3100, ext 7100 🕐 Tue–Sat 10–5 (to 6 early June–late Aug) 🎫 Free 🚇 Monorail

KERRY PARK VIEWPOINT

seattle.gov

Visit this tiny park on Queen Anne Hill with great views.

🔶 A10 ✉ 211 W Highland Drive ☎ 206/684-4075 🕐 Daily 6–10 🚌 2

KEYARENA

keyarena.com

The arena is home to many sports teams, including the Seattle Storm and Seattle University Redhawks basketball teams. It also hosts big-name stadium concerts and shows.

🔶 B12 ✉ Seattle Center ☎ 206/584-7200 🚌 1, 2, 3, 4, 24 to Seattle Center 🚇 Monorail

SEATTLE CENTER MONORAIL

seattlemonorail.com

It takes riders past major sights between Westlake Center and Seattle Center every ten minutes.

🔶 C13 ✉ Seattle Center station: next to the Space Needle. Westlake Center station: at 5th Avenue and Pine Street ☎ 206/905-2620 🕐 Mon–Fri 7.30am–11pm, Sat–Sun 8.30am–11pm 🦽 Good 🎫 Inexpensive

SEATTLE CHILDREN'S MUSEUM

thechildrensmuseum.org

Visit an African village or create enormous soap bubbles here.

🔶 B12 ✉ The Armory/Center House, first level, 305 Harrison Street, Seattle Center ☎ 206/441-1768 🕐 Tue–Fri 10–5, Sat–Sun 10–6 🚌 3, 4 🚇 Monorail 🎫 Moderate

SEATTLE CHILDREN'S THEATRE

sct.org

Recognized worldwide, the SCT is a prized cultural resource for families.

🔶 B12 ✉ 201 St. Thomas Street, Seattle Center ☎ 206/441-3322 🕐 Performances Sep to mic-May Fri–Sun 🚌 1, 2, 3, 4, 16 to Seattle Center 🚇 Monorail

The nighttime view of the city from Kerry Park, seen through the sculpture

Lovely Streets of Queen Anne

From the lively neighborhood of lower Queen Anne to the peaceful neighborhoods of the upper hill, take in the views of Seattle's skyline.

DISTANCE: 4 miles (6.25km) **ALLOW:** 2.25 hours

START

DICK'S DRIVE-IN
🚏 B11 🚌 1, 2, 8, 13

END

HILLTOP ALE HOUSE
🚏 A8 🚌 3, 4, 13

1 Start at Dick's Drive-In (on the corner of Republican Street and Queen Anne Avenue N), a quintessential Seattle fast-food joint serving burgers, hand-cut fries and old-fashioned milkshakes.

8 Stroll south along Queen Anne Avenue N, which is lined with shops, restaurants and bars. Stop for a beverage at the Hilltop Ale House.

2 Leave Dick's and walk east on Republican Street for two blocks. Enter the Seattle Center campus, with the Seattle Repertory Theatre (▷ 55) and the Pacific Northwest Ballet (▷ 55) on your left.

7 Go north on 7th Avenue W to West McGraw Street. Turn right, grab a coffee and a pastry at the Macrina Bakery (▷ 43), and continue on for seven blocks to Queen Anne Avenue N.

3 On your right you'll see the International Fountain, a favorite spot on warm days. Southeast lies Armory/Center House and its food court.

6 Turn left on W Highland Drive. Walk two blocks to Kerry Park for views of Mount Rainier and the Space Needle (▷ 52). Continue west on W Highland Drive.

4 Walk west along the southern edge of KeyArena (▷ 53). Continue west to Queen Anne Avenue N. Turn right, go north to Roy Street, then take a soft left turn up the hill on West Queen Anne Driveway.

5 Continue on this street onto 1st Avenue W. There's an imposing hill for a few blocks, but the views are fine.

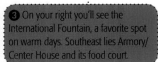

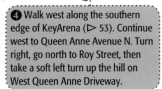

Shopping

LUNA SANDALS

lunasandals.com

Locally made minimalist sandals for men, women and children that are customizable. Their design is based on recycled tire shoes.

➕ C11 ✉ 817 5th Avenue N ☎ 855/586-2726 🕐 Mon–Thu 10–5, Fri 10–4

METROPOLITAN MARKET

metropolitan-market.com

High-end grocery store based in Seattle that sells many locally produced fare, from artisan breads and smelly cheeses to wines, coffees and seafood

delicacies, so it's great for getting edible souvenirs, and a ready-made meal. There's a great flower shop, too.

➕ B11 ✉ 100 Mercer Street ☎ 206/213-0778 🕐 Daily 24 hours

ONCE UPON A TIME

onceuponatimeseattle.com

Charming children's store located in a restored Victorian home at the top of the hill. Wonderful selection of wooden toys, beautiful clothing and puzzles, plus regular themed community events.

➕ B9 1622 ✉ Queen Anne Avenue N ☎ 206/284-7260 🕐 Mon–Sat 9–6, Sun 11–5

Entertainment and Nightlife

THE MASONRY

themasonryseattle.com

Small, industrial-designed bar with an extensive bottled craft beer list plus a dozen or more on tap. Some of the best Neapolitan-style pizza in the city and great meatballs, both made in the wood-burning oven.

➕ B11 ✉ 201 Mercer Street, Seattle Center ☎ 206/441-7178 🚌 1, 2, 13

ON THE BOARDS

ontheboards.org

Contemporary performing arts theater for dance, performance artists, and musical talents from all over the world.

➕ A11 ✉ 20 Roy Street ☎ 206/453-4375 🚌 2, 13, 29

PACIFIC NORTHWEST BALLET

pnb.org

Renowned company under the direction

of former New York City Ballet dancers.

➕ B11 ✉ Performances are at McCaw Hall at 321 Mercer Street ☎ 206/441-9411 🚌 2, 3, 4, 8, 13, 29

SEATTLE OPERA

seattleopera.org

One of the pre-eminent opera companies, with four or five productions September through May.

➕ B11 ✉ Performances at McCaw Hall, 321 Mercer Street, Seattle Center ☎ 206/389-7676 🚌 1, 2, 13

SEATTLE REPERTORY THEATER

seattlerep.org

Known locally as The Rep, this well-established, award-winning theater has been showing a diverse range of plays and musicals since 1963.

➕ B11 ✉ 155 Mercer Street ☎ 206/443-2222 🚌 2, 13, 29

Where to Eat

PRICES	
Prices are approximate, based on a 3-course meal for one person.	
$$$	over $50
$$	$30–$50
$	under $30

5 SPOT ($)

chowfoods.com

An ever-changing menu from different regions: You never know if you'll get Creole catfish or New England clam chowder.

➕ A9 ✉ 1502 Queen Anne Avenue N ☎ 206/285-7768 🕐 Breakfast, lunch and dinner daily

BETTY ($$)

eatatbetty.com

Casual bistro with a refined, seasonal menu of traditional American fare and French comfort food. Try their Oven Roasted Chicken or the Steak Frites.

➕ A9 ✉ 1507 Queen Anne Avenue N ☎ 206/352-3773 🕐 Dinner daily

CROW ($$)

eatatcrow.com

Large, airy restaurant with kitchen-bar seating and a classic and well-done menu with favorites such as steamed mussels, roasted chicken and lasagna.

➕ C10 ✉ 823 5th Avenue N ☎ 206/283-8800 🕐 Dinner daily

EDEN HILL ($$$)

edenhillrestaurant.com

Red brick outside, quaint and intimate inside, with a seasonal and local, avant-garde menu. The best way to explore this is through the Chef's Tasting menu, but leave room for dessert.

➕ Off map ✉ 2209 Queen Anne Avenue N ☎ 206/708-6836 🕐 Dinner Tue–Sun

MASHAWI ($$)

mashawirestaurant.com

Generous portions of delicious Lebanese specialties, favoured by the theater crowd. Try the Zahra—deep fried cauliflower that even the kids will love.

➕ C11 ✉ 366 Roy Street ☎ 206/282-0078 🕐 Lunch Wed–Fri, dinner daily

SKYCITY AT THE NEEDLE ($$$)

At 500ft (152m), this newly renovated restaurant with 360 degree city views has a first-of-its-kind rotating glass floor, revealing stunning downward views and the mechanics of the turntable.

➕ C12 ✉ 400 Broad Street (in the Space Needle) ☎ 206/905-2100 🕐 Lunch and dinner daily, brunch on weekends

TACOS CHUKIS ($)

Casual taqueria known for its excellent tacos, baby burritos and *nopal asado* (grilled cactus). Take it to go and eat it a few blocks east overlooking Lake Union.

➕ D10 ✉ 832 Dexter Avenue N ☎ 206/248-9317 🕐 Lunch and dinner daily

TOULOUSE PETIT ($$)

toulousepetit.com

Ornate, candle-lit Creole restaurant that's equally great for brunch as it is for dinner. Their *beignets* (dougnuts) are wonderful, as is their traditional gumbo.

➕ A11 ✉ 601 Queen Anne Avenue N ☎ 206/432-9069 🕐 Breakfast, lunch and dinner daily

WINDY CITY PIE ($)

windycitypie.com

Conveniently located inside a distillery, this eatery serves Chicago-style deep-dish pizza with some unusual toppings.

➕ Off map ✉ 1417 Elliott Avenue W ☎ 206/486-4743 🕐 Lunch Sat–Sun, dinner daily

The Capitol Hill neighborhood is colorful and diverse, buzzing with bars and bistros, vintage theaters and independent shops. It's also the city's LGBTQ hub. To the north-east lies Washington Park, with it's wide, tree-lined streets and 19th-century houses.

Capitol Hill

HIGHLIGHTS

● Volunteer Park (▷ 67)
and its 1912 conservatory
● Sipping cappuccino at an
authentic coffeehouse
● Letting loose at carnival-
themed bar Unicorn
● Shopping for vintage
clothing on Broadway
● Dining at a romantic
bistro

TIP

● Walk to the Hill from
Downtown—it's less than a
20-minute stroll, and parking can be nightmarish.

As Seattle's counterculture neighborhood,
Capitol Hill is continually evolving and
offers a bit of everything, including iconic
bookstores, independent coffee shops,
eclectic restaurants, and some of the city's
best nightlife.

A street scene The stretch of Broadway
between Roy Street (at the north end) and
Madison Street (at the south end) is home to
an impressive array of locally owned coffee-
houses. This lively street pulses with activity at
all hours of day and night. Street performers,
teen punk-rockers and colorful personalities can
be found throughout the mile-long corridor, but
there are two epicenters of activity—the intersection of Broadway and John Street, and the
intersection of Broadway and Pike Street.

Drop in for coffee (top left) or lie back and relax with a massage (top middle) after a hard day's sightseeing in the Capitol Hill district; the annual PrideFest takes place through Capitol Hill (bottom left); a statue on Broadway celebrates one of the city's most famous sons, Jimi Hendrix (right)

Taverns, bars and clubs The Hill, as it's affectionately known, is a destination nightspot. Party seekers come from miles around—often from across Lake Washington—to drink, dance and revel in the area's endless array of dive bars, upscale lounges and pulsating dance clubs. (The Pike/Pine corridor alone is loaded with bars and clubs, both gay and straight.)

Breathing space For fresh air and open spaces, head to Cal Anderson Park, one of the nation's loveliest public parks. Named after Washington's first openly gay legislator, the park has plenty of things to do and features grassy lawns for picnics, a fountain, wading pools, a children's play area, an oversized chess board, tennis courts, and a water tower that you can climb for great views of Downtown.

THE BASICS

H10

8, 9, 11, 43, 47, 49

Lake Union

Life by the water (left) and kayaking (right) on Lake Union; Route 99 bridge (far right)

THE BASICS

- E9
- 42, 62, 70
- South Lake Union Streetcar from Westlake
- Argosy Cruises (▷ 118); Ride the Ducks tours (ridetheducksofseattle.com); Seattle Seaplanes (▷ 118)

DID YOU KNOW?

- In the 1950s, Seattle had over 2,500 floating homes. Now it's down to about 500.
- Lake Union took its name from a pioneer's speech in which he dreamed that one day a lake would form "the union" between Puget Sound and Lake Washington.
- Gas Works Park, on the north side, offers great views of Downtown.

Waterfront walkways, historic ships, and science and tech companies surround this neighborhood, while the lake itself provides a recreational space for kayakers, sailboats, seaplanes and houseboats.

Floating world The houseboat life started more than a century ago on Lake Union. A sawmill that opened on the lake in 1881 attracted a community of loggers and their hangers-on. Many of these woodsmen built makeshift shelters by tying felled logs together and erecting tarpaper shacks on top. Before long, thousands of shacks floated on the waterways. These "floating homes" were Seattle's earliest houseboats, and a far cry from the versions made familiar by the film *Sleepless in Seattle*.

Boats and stores Today Lake Union is a lively mix of marine activity, houseboat living and expensive dining and shopping. Start your visit with a stroll, passing the Center for Wooden Boats on the south end, to get right into the seafaring spirit. Then, for a true Lake Union experience, go out on the lake. You can rent sailboats, skiffs or kayaks, and explore on your own, or sign on with a tour. Back ashore, there are the numerous good restaurants on Chandler's Cove.

Seaplane central The Lake is also a bustling aquatic airport; Kenmore Air operates numerous flights to and from Lake Union daily. Sightseeing flights are available, too.

Washington Park Arboretum

TOP 25

● The Arboretum covers an area of 230 acres (93ha).
● Botanist Edmond S. Meany test-planted imported seeds in his own garden, and later transplanted the plants on campus.

This large botanical collection owes its origins to Edmond S. Meany, founder of the University of Washington's School of Environmental and Forest Sciences. Today's garden combines exotics with virtually every woodland plant indigenous to the area.

Green oasis Meany initiated a seed exchange with universities around the world. As a result, you can walk through a variety of ecological zones and enjoy a rich diversity of flora.

The Japanese Garden Tucked within the south end of the Arboretum lies the restful Japanese Garden. The garden was designed in 1960 by Juki Lida, a Tokyo landscape architect, who personally supervised both its planning and

Blossom-covered shrubs adorn the water's edge of the Japanese Garden

construction. Elements of the garden—plants, trees, water, rocks—and their placement represent a miniature world of mountain, forest, lake, river and tableland. There's also a ceremonial teahouse where visitors can reserve a place and experience the tranquil, 40-minute Way of Tea ceremony seated on tatami mats.

Waterfront Trail The Arboretum provides miles of interpretive trails that are well marked. Created in the 1930s, Azalea Way is one of the best trails to walk along, as it's a level, just under a mile (1.5km) walkway through the heart of the park. Planted on either side of the wide walkway are azaleas, dogwoods, magnolias and other companion plants, all set against a backdrop of evergreen trees. In the spring, the flowering cherry trees are spectacular.

THE BASICS

botanicgardens.uw.edu (Arboretum)
seattlejapanesegarden.org (Japanese Garden)

✚ K8

✉ 2300 Arboretum Drive E (Graham Visitor Center) 1075 Lake Washington Boulevard E (Japanese Garden)

☎ 206/543-8800; Japanese Garden 206/684-4725

🕐 Daily dawn–dusk; Japanese Garden Mar–Sep daily; Oct–Feb Tue–Sun

🚌 11

♿ Some

🎫 Free except the Japanese Garden, which has a small admission price

65

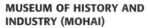

More to See

CHAPEL OF ST. IGNATIUS

seattleu.edu/chapel/

This sublime chapel is Seattle University's architectural gift to the city. Architect Steven Holl visualized the structure as "seven bottles of light in a stone box," with light bouncing off the tinted baffles to create a halo effect on the surrounding walls.

🕂 G14 ✉ 901 12th Avenue, near Marion Street on Capitol Hill ☎ 206/296-6075 🕐 Mon–Thu 7am–10pm, Fri 7–7, Sat 8–5, Sun 8am–10pm. Regular liturgies 🚌 2, 12

LAKE VIEW CEMETERY

lakeviewcemeteryassociation.com

Situated atop Capitol Hill, this beautiful, independent non-profit cemetery was incorporated just seven years after the end of the Civil War and Seattle's pioneers are buried here. However, it is the graves of martial arts cult star Bruce Lee (near the top of the hill) and his son, Brandon, that draw visitors.

🕂 G9 ✉ 1554 15th Avenue E at E Garfield, Capitol Hill 🚌 10

MUSEUM OF HISTORY AND INDUSTRY (MOHAI)

mohai.org

With space to display its iconic items from Seattle's past and to regularly add history-in-the-making exhibits, this is a lively and engaging place. The Bezos Center for Innovation reflects the range of items, ideas, and projects from the local area. Maritime Seattle explores the city's relationship with the sea, including a working periscope to view the city. Perhaps the most engaging exhibit of all is True Northwest: The Seattle Journey, which traces the settlement and development of the area through a series of displays, each combining artifacts and images of a particular era with interactive devices. Temporary exhibitions explore aspects of the city in greater detail.

🕂 D10 ✉ 860 Terry Avenue N ☎ 206/324-1126 🕐 Daily 10–5 (to 8 Thu) 🚊 South Lake Union Streetcar from Westlake Center Park 🚻 Excellent 💰 Moderate, free 1st Thu of month

Inside the lofty main hall at the Museum of History and Industry

The Museum of History and Industry occupies a historic building on South Lake Union

PHOTOGRAPHIC CENTER NORTHWEST

pcnw.org

Modern and bright space that's both a gallery and photography school, with one-day public workshops on offer for all skill levels.

➕ G14 ✉ 900 12th Avenue ☎ 206/720-7222 🕐 Mon–Thu 12–9, Sat–Sun 12–6 🚌 2, 12 ♿ Some accessibility

REI

rei.com

This is the flagship store for Seattle's premier co-op retailer of outdoor clothing and equipment, where you can try before you buy. Rock-climbing, gear rentals and bike repairs are on offer.

➕ E12 ✉ 222 Yale Avenue N ☎ 206/223-1944 🕐 Mon–Sat 9–9, Sun 10–7 🚌 304, 355 ♿ Good accessibility

STIMSON-GREEN MANSION

preservewa.org

Completed in 1901, this is a splendid example of an English Tudor Revival-style home on the outside, with an eclectic mix of other architectural styles inside, including Gothic and Renaissance. Tours by The Washington Trust are $10.

➕ F14 ✉ 1204 Minor Avenue ☎ 206/624-0474 🚌 2, 63, 64 🕐 Tours are on 2nd Tue of every month, 1–2.30 ♿ Some accessibility

VOLUNTEER PARK

seattle.gov

Volunteer Park was named during the Spanish-American War of 1898 to honor those who had served as soldiers. The park offers more than green space. There's a water tower to climb for 360-degree views or stroll through the conservatory to admire the botanical environments from around the world. The grand art deco building is home to the Seattle Asian Art Museum (currently under renovation).

➕ G10 ✉ 1247 15th Avenue E ☎ 206/684-4075 🕐 Park daily 6am–10pm. Conservatory Tue–Sun 10–4 🚌 10, 49 💵 Conservatory is inexpensive and free on 1st Thu and Sat of month ♿ Good

Black Sun *(Isamu Noguchi, 1969), a sculpture in Volunteer Park*

A Walk in Washington Park Arboretum

Visit Seattle's woodsy urban paradise and walk through a wetland trail, viewing the city's flora and fauna in its natural habitat.

DISTANCE: 4.25 miles (7km) **ALLOW:** 2.5 hours

START

24TH AVENUE E AND E CALHOUN STREET
✚ J7 🚌 43, 48

1 From the bus stop, go north on 24th Avenue E, turn right on E Calhoun Street for one block, left on 25th Avenue E, then right on E Miller Street to enter the park. Turn right on Lake Washington Boulevard E, then left on E Foster Island Road.

2 Join the Waterfront Trail at the water's edge. Follow the trail over bridges, across waterways and through wetlands to Foster island.

3 Take note of the bird life—specifically red-winged blackbirds, goldfinches and Canada geese. Turn left at the conclusion of the Waterfront Trail.

4 Take the path that leads to the tip of Foster Island, for views of Union Bay and Husky Stadium (▷ 81). Backtrack before crossing under the big noisy highway 520.

END

24TH AVENUE E AND E CALHOUN STREET
✚ J6 🚌 43, 48

8 Various side paths off Arboretum Drive E allow you to explore themed plantings that include native Pacific species, rhododendrons, magnolias and maples, before leading you back to the Graham Visitor Center. From here follow Foster Island Road and retrace your steps to the bus stop.

7 When you come to the end of Azalea Way, turn left onto Lake Washington Boulevard E, passing the Japanese Garden (▷ 64), then go left again on Arboretum Drive E.

6 From the Visitor Center, walk south along Azalea Way, a grass walkway that leads through the heart of the Arboretum (▷ 64).

5 The path leads to the Arboretum's Graham Visitor Center. Stop here for a bathroom break or to admire the gardens and gift shop.

Shopping

ELLIOTT BAY BOOK COMPANY

elliottbaybook.com

A Seattle institution, this independent bookstore hosts free readings by top authors. The café serves a great brunch.
⊞ G13 ✉ 1521 10th Avenue ☎ 206/624-6600 or 800/962-5311 ⏰ Mon–Thu 10–10, Fri–Sat 10am–11pm, Sun 10–9

GHOST GALLERY

ghostgalleryshop.com

Funky jewelry, clothing, perfume, wire, and affordable art from local artists are found here at this neat little gallery.
⊞ F12 ✉ 504 Denny Way by Hillcrest Market ⏰ Wed–Fri 11–7, Sat–Sun 11–6

LE FROCK VINTAGE

lefrockonline.com

Recycled and vintage clothing for men and women, and designer samples.
⊞ F13 ✉ 613 E Pike Street ☎ 206/623-5339 ⏰ Mon–Sat 10–7, Sun 12–6

LIKELIHOOD

likelihood.us

Ultra modern-looking boutique selling fashionable sneakers for men and women. Adidas, Converse, New Balance, Nike, Puma, Vans, and a host of high-end brands can be found here.
⊞ G14 ✉ 1101 E Union Street ☎ 206/257-0577 ⏰ Mon–Thu 11–7, Fri–Sat 11–8, Sun 11–6

MELROSE MARKET

melrosemarketseattle.com

Smaller, but no less enjoyable than Pike Place Market, this open food and retail market occupies a set of historic automotive buildings from the 1920s.
⊞ F13 ✉ 1531 Melrose Avenue ⏰ Daily

Entertainment and Nightlife

OPTIMISM BREWING COMPANY

optimismbrewing.com

Spacious venue with a dozen craft beers on tap, a play area for kids, a patio, and food trucks parked right outside.
⊞ G14 ✉ 1158 Broadway ☎ 206/651-5429

ROCK BOX

rockboxseattle.com

Enjoy karaoke with only your chosen party looking on, in one of the private rooms at this Japanese-style venue.
⊞ G13 ✉ 1603 Nagle Place
☎ 206/302-7625 ⏰ Mon–Wed 4pm–2am, Thu 4pm–3am, Fri–Sat 3pm–4am, Sun 3pm–2am

SIFF CINEMA EGYPTIAN

siff.net

An art-house single-screen theater showing independent films with some balcony seating available. Beer and wine can be purchased from the concession stand, as well as the usual popcorn.
⊞ F13 ✉ 805 E Pine Street ☎ 206/324-9996

FILM

Seattle is a great place for film buffs. The city hosts the annual Seattle International Film Festival (SIFF) in May and June. Other film festivals include Cinema Italian Style, French Cinema Now, and Noir City.

Where to Eat

ALTURA ($$$)

alturarestaurant.com

The daily-changing menu of artistically
presented Italian dishes is likely to
include seasonal wild ingredients alongside local heirloom items.

🔢 G11 ✉ 617 Broadway E ☎ 206/402-6749
🕓 Dinner Tue–Sat

ARAYA'S PLACE ($)

arayasplace.com

Vegan Thai food is served buffet-style at
lunch and from the large menu at
dinner.

🔢 K11 ✉ 2808 E Madison Street
☎ 206/402-6634 🕓 Lunch and dinner daily

CAFÉ PRESSE ($)

cafepresseseattle.com

European-inspired coffee and cuisine.
Full bar with excellent cocktails; televised
international soccer on weekends.

🔢 G14 ✉ 1117 12th Avenue ☎ 206/709-
7674 🕓 Breakfast, lunch and dinner daily

CAFFÈ LADRO ($)

caffeladro.com

Wooden chairs line the front of this
friendly neighborhood coffee shop.

🔢 A11 ✉ 435 15th Avenue E ☎ 206/267-
0551 🕓 Daily 5.30am–8pm

ESPRESSO VIVACE ($)

espressovivace.com

The best place to get a cup of coffee in
the city, with umbrella-shaded tables;
perfect for people-watching.

🔢 G12 ✉ 532 Broadway Avenue E
☎ 206/860-2722 🕓 Daily 6am–11pm

NUE ($$)

nueseattle.com

Ever-changing street-food inspired small
plates from around the globe.

🔢 H13 ✉ 1519 14th Avenue ☎ 206/257-
0312 🕓 Lunch and dinner daily

PINE BOX ($)

pineboxbar.com

With a commitment to local, ethically-
sourced ingredients, this pub serves
good soups, sandwiches and pizzas.

🔢 F13 ✉ 1600 Melrose Avenue
☎ 206/588-0375 🕓 Dinner daily, brunch
Sat–Sun

QUEEN BEE CAFÉ ($)

queenbeecafe.com

The delicious soups, salads and home-
baked crumpets are sure to entice you
in; all its profits go to local charities, too.

🔢 J12 ✉ 2200 E Madison Street, Suite B
☎ 206/757-6314 🕓 Mon–Fri 7–4, Sat–Sun
7–5

SERAFINA ($$)

serafinaseattle.com

Rustic Italian cuisine by candlelight, and
an outdoor deck for summer.

🔢 F8 ✉ 2043 Eastlake Avenue E
☎ 206/323-0807 🕓 Lunch Mon–Fri,
dinner nightly

TANGO ($$)

tangorestaurant.com

Latin cuisine in a chic but cozy atmosphere. Try the tapas, the paella, or their
famous El Diablo dessert—a bittersweet
cube of dark, spicy chocolate with burnt
meringue and a tequila caramel sauce.

🔢 F13 ✉ 1100 Pike Street ☎ 206/583-0382
🕓 Dinner nightly

University District

The U District is a great mix of residential streets, urban avenues and roomy campus quadrangles. Its best-known attraction is University Way, a vibrant boulevard lined with eateries, cafés and shops.

North East 52nd Street

East

East

East

North

East

NORTH STREET

North

North

North

North

Dalsey Street North East

NORTH

East 47th Street

AVENUE

North Avenue

East

Avenue

22nd Avenue

Avenue

Ravenna

NORTH AVENUE

25TH AVENUE

20th Avenue

21st

UNIVERSITY DISTRICT

15TH

17TH

18th

19th

University Village Shopping Center

NORTH EAST 45TH STREET

Burke Museum of Natural History and Culture

EAST

Whitman Court North East

Walla Walla Road

E Stevens Way North East

513

NORTH

Memorial Way North East

P

Pend Oreille Road North East

P

AVENUE

Henry Art Gallery

University of Washington

E Stevens Way North East

NORTH EAST

P

Walla Walla Road

15TH

Meany Hall

Red Square

Mason Road North East

Canal Road

Suzzallo & Allen Library

Jefferson Road North East

BOULEVARD

Drumheller Fountain

MONTLAKE

Intramural Activities

Conibear Shellhouse

W Stevens Way North East

Edmundson Pavilion

NORTH EAST PACIFIC STREET

NORTH EAST PACIFIC PLACE

Husky Stadium

Columbia Road

University Medical Center

University of Washington Station

San Juan Road

P

P

UW Waterfront Activities Center

MONTLAKE BRIDGE

Lake Washington Ship Canal   (Montlake Cut)

H

J

K

University District

Burke Museum of Natural History and Culture

The Burke's permanent collection demonstrates a genuine respect for the cultural traditions of featured groups and a scientist's attention to detail.

The Burke's beginnings The museum's origins date back to 1879, when four enthusiastic teenagers calling themselves the Young Naturalists' Society set about collecting Northwest plant and animal specimens, a popular hobby at the time. Their collection grew, so much that to house it a museum was built on the University of Washington campus in 1885. Over the next 20 years, the number of specimens increased, and today they form the basis of the Burke's vast collection. A new building is under construction on the northwest corner of the UW campus, due to open in 2019.

With its origins dating back to 1879, the Burke Museum has amassed a huge collection of more than 16 million objects, including the skeletal remains of a dinosaur (left, bottom middle) and early arrowheads (left middle); children are fascinated by the Bug Blast Exhibition (top right) and love to examine the old bones (bottom right)

Treasures on display As you walk through the entrance, a stunning glass display case demands immediate attention. It highlights selected treasures from this vast collection, and gives you an idea of what's in store. In the halls beyond, two exhibits showcase the museum's strong suits: natural history and ethnography. The Pacific Voices exhibit conveys the variety of Pacific Rim cultures, from New Zealand to the northwest coast of Canada. By framing the exhibit around the celebrations and rituals that are central to each culture, museum objects are placed within their appropriate context. Constructed "sets," photo murals, sounds and informative text communicate the importance of cultural traditions. The Life and Times of Washington State exhibit is a chronological journey through 545 million years of Washington history.

THE BASICS

burkemuseum.org

✚ H3

✉ UW campus at NE 45th Street and 17th Avenue NE

☎ 206/616-3962

🕐 Daily 10–5 (1st Thu of month until 8)

🍴 Burke Café

🚌 43, 68, 70, 71, 72, 73

♿ Very good

💲 Moderate. Free on 1st Thu of month

Henry Art Gallery

James Turrell's Skyspace, Light Reign, exhibit (left); one of the contemporary galleries (right)

THE BASICS

henryart.org

✚ H4

✉ UW campus at 15th Avenue NE and NE 41st Street

☎ 206/543-2280

🕐 Wed–Sun 11–4 (Thu until 9)

🍴 City Grind

🚌 25, 43, 70, 71, 72, 73

♿ Very good

💵 Moderate; free Sun and 1st Thu of month

HIGHLIGHTS

● The Monsen Collection of Photography
● Regular artists' lectures, symposia and film showings

TIPS

● Experience Skyspace, Light Reign, at different times of the day, especially after dark with its intense spectrum of LED lights.
● Every month a free, special family-friendly ArtVenture is hosted.

The Henry Art Gallery, dedicated to contemporary art, collects and encourages artists to produce thought-provoking works, and invites visitors to discover the power of their innovative imagery.

The gallery The art museum of the University of Washington has 14,000sq ft (1,302sq m) of gallery space and includes an auditorium, education studio and sculpture court, with the elliptical *Skyspace* by the artist James Turrell.

Skyspace, *Light Reign* The piece is the first installation of its kind to combine two key aspects of Turrell's work: skyspace and exterior architectural illumination. It provides both a meditative gallery experience and a public art component that can be viewed from outside the museum.

The collection A cornerstone of the collection is the Monsen Collection of Photography, from vintage prints to contemporary explorations of the medium. The permanent collection also includes 19th- to 20th-century landscape paintings, modern art by Stuart Davis, Robert Motherwell and Lionel Feininger, and the international Costume and Textile Collection, exhibited on a rotating basis.

Learn as you go In addition to films, lectures and tours, the museum presents discussions of a current exhibition and outlines how an exhibition is developed.

University of Washington

The University campus entrance (left); students gather on the steps bordering Red Square (right)

The University campus was originally planned as a fairground for Seattle's 1909 Exposition celebrating the Alaska Gold Rush. Much of the design, including Rainier Vista, has been preserved.

Vistas and fountains To begin your tour stop at the visitor information center to pick up a free self-guided tour map and an events schedule. As you walk, you'll see buildings in a variety of architectural styles, from turreted Denny Hall to cathedral-like Suzzallo & Allen Library. The Suzzallo & Allen faces Red Square, a student gathering place. Only the *Broken Obelisk* sculpture and three campanile towers break the horizontal line of this plaza, which is bordered by Meany Hall, a performing arts venue.

Elsewhere To the west lies the Henry Art Gallery (▷ 76). To the north, the old campus quadrangle is especially inviting in late March, when rows of pink Japanese cherry trees burst into bloom. Continuing toward the university's north entrance, you come to the Burke Museum (▷ 74–75) and UW's observatory (▷ 81). Head toward the Waterfront Activities Center (▷ 78) to rent a canoe.

The Ave One block west of the campus lies University Way NE, known as "the Ave." Here, a multitude of ethnic restaurants, bookstores, cafés, and secondhand stores share the avenue with college kids who call the neighborhood "home."

THE BASICS

washington.edu

⊞ H4

✉ Between 15th and 25th avenues, NE and Campus Parkway and NE 45th Street; The UW Visitor Center is located in the basement of the Odegaard Undergraduate Library.

☎ 206/543-9198

🕐 Mon–Fri 8–5

🚌 25, 43, 70, 71, 72, 73

♿ Good

DID YOU KNOW?

● The university moved to its present location in 1895.
● Most locals call the university "U Dub."
● Suzzallo & Allen Library was modeled after King's College Chapel in Cambridge, England.
● Husky Stadium has seats for 70,083 people.

TIP

● Rent a canoe or rowboat at the University's Waterfront Activities Center; you can paddle across the Montlake Cut to the Washington Park Arboretum (▷ 64–65).

More to See

A SOUND GARDEN

wrc.noaa.gov

One of Seattle's small treasures and one of six public art works on the NOAA campus. Doug Hollis's ingenious sculpture consists of 12 steel towers with wind-activated organ pipes that create gentle sounds on windy days. Restricted access and photo ID required.

🔁 Off map at J3 ✉ Behind NOAA building, 7600 Sand Point Way NE ⏰ Mon–Fri 9–5, last entry 3.30pm 🚌 74, 75

UNIVERSITY DISTRICT FARMERS' MARKET

seattlefarmersmarkets.org

All the fresh and delicious offerings at this market are locally produced; much of it is organic as well. Pick up the best ingredients for cooking at home, or eat right at the market. From breakfast sandwiches and pastries, to *tamales*, fries and yogurt, there are lots of ready-made options on offer.

🔁 H2 ✉ University Way NE and NE 50th Street ⏰ Sat 9–2 🚌 45, 70, 71, 73, 74

UW CENTER FOR URBAN HORTICULTURE

botanicgardens.uw.edu

Founded in 1984, the center includes a variety of garden areas and a 74-acre (30ha) wildlife habitat. Principal attractions include a herbarium and the Union Bay Natural Area, a waterfront open space that is excellent for bird-watching.

🔁 Off map at J3 ✉ 3501 NE 41st Street ☎ 206/543-8616 ⏰ Daily dawn–dusk 🚌 25, 65, 75

UW WATERFRONT ACTIVITIES CENTER

washington.edu

The center sits on the shore of the Montlake Cut, where canoes and rowboats are available for rental to explore the twisting, calm-water channels of the nearby Washington Park Arboretum.

🔁 J6 ✉ 3710 Montlake Boulevard NE, on Union Bay, behind Husky Stadium ☎ 206/543-9433 ⏰ Center: daily; rentals: Apr–Oct 🚌 25, 43, 65, 67, 68

University District Farmers' Market

Waterfront Activities Center

Through Campus and Beyond

Stroll through UW's picturesque campus and visit a host of renowned University-affiliated institutions.

DISTANCE: 2.5 miles (6.25km) **ALLOW:** 1.5 hours

START

UNIVERSITY BOOK STORE (▷ 80)
✚ H3 🚍 45, 70, 71, 73, 74

1 Begin by browsing the immense selection of books at the University Book Store (▷ 80), a local treasure that hosts daily events.

2 Leave the bookstore through the east exit, turn right and walk south to NE 43rd Street. Turn left and cross 15th Avenue NE, entering the UW campus (▷ 77).

3 Walk uphill to the Burke Museum (▷ 74–75) and view its comprehensive collection of regional objects. From the Burke, walk south on Memorial Way NE, then George Washington Lane NE to the Henry Art Gallery (▷ 76).

4 Visit the Henry's impressive contemporary art. Grab a snack in the cafe. Upon leaving the gallery, walk east into Red Square, the brick-paved central plaza of the campus.

END

UNIVERSITY BOOK STORE
✚ H3 🚍 45, 70, 71, 73, 74

8 Depart the café and walk north for six blocks on University Way NE to the University Book Store.

7 Follow W Stevens Way NE until it intersects with NE 40th Street. Turn left on NE 40th Street and walk to University Way NE. Then turn left again, walking downhill for two long blocks to Agua Verde (▷ 82) on NE Boat Street. Enjoy margaritas and tortas on the deck, while taking in the view of Portage Bay and its resident houseboats.

6 Continue to the Drumheller Fountain, which offers a good view of Mt. Rainier (▷ 105). Continue southeast (still downhill) and turn right on W Stevens Way NE.

5 Stop to admire the Gothic facade of the Suzzallo & Allen Library before heading downhill to the southeast.

UNIVERSITY DISTRICT WALK

Shopping

BULLDOG NEWS

bulldognews.com

A newsstand on steroids, this neighborhood hangout has all the latest arts, lifestyle, business and sports publications. The on-site espresso bar is also excellent.

H3 ✉ 4208 University Way NE
☎ 206/632-6397 ⏰ Mon–Fri 6.30am–7pm, Sat–Sun 8–7 🚌 45, 71, 73

HARDWICK'S HARDWARE

ehardwicks.com

Unique, family owned and operated store since 1932, where aisles are stuffed with good-quality tools, strange gizmos and useful gadgets. Great for any DIY products or just to browse around.

G4 ✉ 4214 Roosevelt Way NE
☎ 206/632-1203 ⏰ Mon–Fri 8–6, Sat 9–6
🚌 65, 67, 74

MAGNUS BOOKS

magnusbooksseattle.com

Solid, independent bookstore, open since the 1970s, with used and out-of-print titles, rare treasures, and helpful, friendly staff.

H4 ✉ 1408 NE 42nd Street ☎ 206/633-1800 🚌 44, 48, 49

NEPTUNE MUSIC COMPANY

Located beneath the Neptune Theatre, this store is one of the few surviving vinyl record stores in the city. Retro tech fans will find loads of movies on VHS as well.

H3 ✉ 4344 Brooklyn Avenue NE
☎ 206/632-0202 🚌 44, 49, 70

SHIGA'S IMPORTS

shigasimports.com

Long-standing, historic Asian gift shop filled with mostly Japanese imports including kimonos, teas, bamboo products, linens and ceramics.

H3 ✉ 4306 University Way NE
☎ 206/633-2400 🚌 45, 71, 73

UNIVERSITY BOOK STORE

ubookstore.com

One of the nation's largest university bookstores. You'll also find Husky apparel (UW football team), laptops and art supplies. Author readings are hosted here, and there's a café for snacks.

H3 ✉ 4326 University Way NE
☎ 206/634-3400 ⏰ Mon–Fri 9–8, Sat 10–7, Sun 12–5 🚌 43, 71, 72, 73

VALLEY OF ROSES

Well-curated vintage shop in what used to be Bruce Lee's old martial arts studio. Clothing, art, books, records, and other treasures are sold here at good prices.

H2 ✉ 4748 University Way NE
☎ 206/522-6887 ⏰ Tue–Sat 12–7
🚌 45, 71, 73, 74, 75

VEGAN HAVEN

veganhaven.org

Nothing in this store has even come close to an animal. You'll find vegan snacks and cookbooks, non-leather belts and wallets, cosmetics and dietary supplements.

Off map ✉ 5270 B University Way NE, corner of 55th ☎ 206/523-9060 ⏰ Daily 10–8 🚌 72, 73

THE WOOLLY MAMMOTH

woollymammothshoes.com

Shoe store with stylish and comfortable brands that are perfect for the Pacific Northwest, including Birkenstock, Blundstone, Chaco, Keen and Merrell.

H3 ✉ 4303 University Way NE
☎ 206/632-3254 ⏰ Mon–Fri 10–7, Sat 10–6, Sun 12–6 🚌 45, 71, 73

Entertainment and Nightlife

BLUE MOON TAVERN

bluemoonseattle.wordpress.com

A local haunt since the 1930s, it's been graced by visits from famous poets such as Theodore Roethke, Dylan Thomas and Allen Ginsberg, among others. Now it's filled with students who appreciate the live music, open mic nights and free peanuts.

✚ G3 ✉ 712 NE 45th Street ☎ 206/675-9116

CHI MAC

Korean-style chicken and beer spot with a simple but effective menu that many students enjoy late into the evening.

✚ H3 ✉ 4525 University Way NE ☎ 206/547-5151

COLLEGE INN PUB

collegeinnpub.com

A bustling basement dive bar that has served college students for decades. The roaring hearth, pool tables and dart boards lend some flavor to the pub's lively atmosphere.

✚ H4 ✉ 4006 University Way NE ☎ 206/634-2307

HUSKY STADIUM

gohuskies.com

The University of Washington's Huskies play PAC-12 football in the fall at the Husky Stadium. Games take place on Saturday.

✚ J5 ✉ Montlake Boulevard NE ☎ 206/543-2200

INTERNATIONAL CHAMBER MUSIC SERIES

meanycenter.org

Renowned chamber music ensembles are performed from fall to spring as part of the University of Washington's "World Series at Meany Hall."

✚ H4 ✉ Meany Theater, University of Washington, 4001 University Way NE ☎ 206/543-4880

JET CITY IMPROV

jetcity.improv.org

Three fast-paced improvised comedy shows appear regularly, including the Twisted Flicks live movie re-dubbing, plus special seasonal shows.

✚ Off map ✉ 5510 University Way NE ☎ 206/352-8291

LITTLE RED HEN

littleredhen.com

A genuine country-and-western bar in the Green Lake neighborhood. Live country music, line dancing, karaoke, beer and snacks.

✚ Off map ✉ 7115 Woodlawn Avenue NE ☎ 206/522-1168

UNIVERSITY OF WASHINGTON OBSERVATORY

washington.edu

The Theodor Jacobsen Observatory was built in 1895 and its 6-inch refracting telescope is still offering celestial views over 120 years later. There's no admission fee and it's open to the public from April till October.

✚ H3 ✉ Entrance to campus at NE 45th Street and 17th Avenue NE ☎ 206/543-2100

BIKE SHARE

The Seattle Department of Transportation (SDOT) is trying several bike-sharing programs in the city. Spin, LimeBike and Ofo are currently operating with their bright neon bicycles. It works by paying and unlocking the bike with an app on your cell phone, and then parking it anywhere, within reason, when you are finished riding. Rates are generally $1/hour.

Where to Eat

PRICES

Prices are approximate, based on a 3-course meal for one person.

$$$	over $50
$$	$30–$50
$	under $30

AGUA VERDE ($)

aguaverde.com

An intimate Mexican-inspired cantina that's on the shore of Portage Bay. Great food, good views and a kayak rental shop downstairs make this a favorite of students.

➕ H5 ✉ 1303 NE Boat Street ☎ 206/545-8570 🕐 Breakfast, lunch and dinner Mon–Sat

AREPA VENEZUELAN KITCHEN ($)

Arepa's can be described as cornbread pita-like sandwiches, which is what is served here at this casual quaint café, and they are delicious. Their *patacones* (thick plantain chips) are great, too.

➕ H3 ✉ 1405 NE 50th Street ☎ 206/556-4879 🕐 Mon–Sat 10.30–8, Sun 11–5

DIE BIERSTUBE ($)

diebierstube.com

An authentic German tavern serving German beers and foods that include bratwurst and *landjäger*.

➕ G2 ✉ 6106 Roosevelt Way NE ☎ 206/527-7019 🕐 Dinner nightly, lunch Sat–Sun

JAK'S GRILL ($$)

jaksgrill.com

Prime, dry-aged steaks, fine Washington wines and a full bar at this standout grill. A favorite post-game destination for well-off Husky fans.

➕ Off map ✉ 3701 NE 45th Street ☎ 206/523-1961 🕐 Tue–Fri, dinner nightly, brunch Sat–Sun

PAIR ($)

pairseattle.com

With a menu of exquisite small plates (including cassoulet Toulouse and smoked salmon toasts), this pint-size bistro is great for a romantic dinner.

➕ Off map ✉ 5501 30th Avenue NE ☎ 206/526-7655 🕐 Dinner Tue–Sat

PORTAGE BAY CAFÉ ($$)

portagebaycafe.com

With an organic menu featuring Dungeness Crab Cake Benedict, Oatmeal Cobbler French Toast and Huevos Rancheros, this is one of the city's most popular breakfast locations.

➕ G4 ✉ 4130 Roosevelt Way NE ☎ 206/547-8230 🕐 Breakfast and lunch daily

SHULTZY'S SAUSAGE ($)

shultzys.com

This modest eatery features their signature sausages, made from high-quality ingredients, plus a rotating menu of beers. Other items include veggie burgers and a chicken sandwich.

➕ H4 ✉ 4114 University Way NE ☎ 206/548-9461 🕐 Lunch and dinner daily

THANH VI ($)

thanhvi.net

Inexpensive, hole-in-the-wall Vietnamese restaurant for authentic, soul-warming *pho* soup and *banh mi* sandwiches, with good vegetarian options here, too.

➕ H3 ✉ 4226 University Way NE ☎ 206/633-7867 🕐 Lunch and dinner daily

VEGGIE GRILL ($)

veggiegrill.com

Vegan fast-food eatery with a selection of nachos, sandwiches, burgers, burritos, tacos and soups on the menu.

➕ K3 ✉ 2681 NE University Village Street ☎ 206/633-1903 🕐 Lunch and dinner daily

Once a warehouse district on the fringes, with a legacy of public art, Fremont's popularity has transformed it in recent years, with high-rises and tech companies moving in. Ballard, too, with its Scandinavian roots and maritime past, is now a hotspot for new restaurants and craft breweries.

50th Street

LAKE WAY

Stone Way North

North

Interlake Avenue North

North 49th Street

North 48th Street

Woodlawn Avenue

Densmore

North 46th Street

NORTH 45TH STREET

Place

WALLINGFORD

North 44th Street

North 43rd Street

Stone Way North

Interlake Avenue

42nd Street

Wallingford Playfield

Woodlawn

Wallingford Avenue

North 34th Street

North

North 43rd Street

North 42nd Street

Burke

Meridian

Bagley

Corliss Avenue

North

North 41st Street

Ashworth

Densmore

NORTH 40TH STREET

North

North

North 39th Street

North

North 38th Street

Way

North

North

North 38th Street

Avenue

Avenue

Avenue

Place

Avenue

Woodlawn

Densmore

Wallingford

Burke

North 37th Street

North 36th Street

Meridian

Bagley

Eastern Avenue North

Corliss Avenue

Sunnyside

Avenue

Avenue

North

North

North

North

PACIFIC STREET

North

Stone

Interlake

Ashworth

Carr

Woodlawn

Densmore

Wallingford

Burke

North 35th Street

Meridian

Bagley

Northlake Way

FREMONT

STREET

North Northlake

NORTH 34TH STREET

Way

● Gas Works Park

Ⓓ   Ⓔ

Fremont and Green Lake Park

HIGHLIGHTS

● Fremont Sunday Market
● Burke-Gilman Trail which follows the old railroad corridor
● Theo Chocolate Factory Tour
● Blooming cherry trees in Green Lake Park in the spring

TIP

The neighborhood's 50 plus public sculptural curiosities can be seen anytime, with the famous Volkswagen-crushing Fremont Troll under Aurora Bridge, and a controversial bronze statue of Lenin being particularly noteworthy.

Fremont, which calls itself "the Center of the Universe," is known for its tolerance and weirdness. It certainly marches to its own beat. Head north 3 miles (4.8km) and you'll find one of Seattle's most beloved green spaces—Green Lake Park

Fremont's past During the 1890s, nearly 5,000 pioneers lived here, many of whom worked in the local mills and on the railroads. Construction of the Aurora Bridge in the 1930s saw an end to the rail service, and the neighborhood began to decline. In the 1960s, Fremont became an artists' mecca due to the low rents and empty warehouse spaces. The 1990s saw yet another transformation with the introduction of high-tech firms moving in, including Adobe Systems Inc.

To get to know Fremont's true character, observe or take part in its many festivals, including the colorful Summer Solstice Parade (left). It is produced by the Fremont Arts Council, and celebrated every June with carnival-style costumes and naked cyclists; family boating on tranquil Green Lake Park (right)

Fremont's future The last two decades have seen other tech companies like Getty Images and Google add Fremont to their headquarters list. The subsequent high-rise construct on followed by a profusion of new restaurants, craft breweries and boutiques, has created a pleasant mix of old and new. Throughout it all, Fremont still retains its free-spirited charm, for now, even if its arty long-time residents hadn't anticipated such a dramatic change.

Green Lake Park Surrounding Green Lake, this nature preserve is a beautiful recreational area for runners, cyclists, swimmers and boaters. The paved trail around the lake is around 3 miles (4.8km). Keep your eyes open for eagles and osprey in the skies, feral rabbits in amongst the bushes, and trout and carp in the water.

THE BASICS
fremont.com
seattle.gov (Green Lake Park)
➕ D6 (Fremont)
✉ 7201 East Green Lake Drive N (Green Lake Park)
☎ 206/632-1500 (Fremont Chamber of Commerce), 206/684-4075 (Green Lake Park)
🚍 5, 26, 28, 31, 32, 40, 62 (Fremont), 26, 45, 62 (Green Lake Park)
♿ Good (Green Lake Park)

Hiram M. Chittenden Locks

TOP
25

DID YOU KNOW?

● Dedicated on July 4, 1917, the Locks were then the second-largest in the world.

● The locks enable vessels to be raised or lowered between 6 and 26ft (2 and 8m), as necessitated by the tides and lake level.

● The average passage through the large lock takes 25 minutes; 10 minutes through the small one.

TIPS

● It can be difficult to get in and out of the parking lot on weekends, but you might find street parking nearby.

● Usually, the peak time for boats to go through the locks is late morning.

Legions of boat owners pass through these locks when taking their boats from freshwater into Puget Sound. Alongside, salmon climb a fish ladder to return to their spawning grounds.

A dream comes true The 1917 opening of the Ballard Locks and Lake Washington Ship Canal was the fulfillment of a 60-year-old pioneer dream to build a channel that would link Lake Washington and Puget Sound. It was Major Hiram M. Chittenden, regional director of the Army Corps of Engineers, that won Congressional approval in 1909 and so work began. Workers excavated and moved thousands of tons of earth with giant steam shovels. Displays in the visitor center explain the history of the locks and ship canal.

Part of the dramatic brushed stainless-steel Salmon Waves sculpture by Paul Storey, which adorns the lock side (left); the locks are operated from a control tower that regulates the spillway gates (below); the fish ladder (bottom right); leisure boats using the sea lock (bottom middle)

Watch the fish A fish ladder, built into the locks, allows salmon and steelheads to move upstream from the sea to their spawning grounds. The fish find the narrow channel and begin the long journey to the freshwater spot where they began life. Here, they lay their eggs and die. There's a viewing window below the waterline, which is open year-round, but if you want to see the most activity visit in the spawning season. Sockeye head this way from about June through mid-August, while chinock and coho salmon follow in September, and you can observe steelheads right through the fall.

Botanical gardens Nearby, you can also explore the 7-acre (3ha) Carl S. English Jr. Botanical Gardens, which are planted with nearly 600 species from around the world.

THE BASICS

ballardlocks.org

🕂 Off map at A2

✉ 3015 NW 54th Street

☎ 206/783-7059

🕓 Locks and gardens: daily 7am–9pm. Visitor center: May–Sep daily 10–6; Oct–Apr Thu–Mon 10–4. Fish Ladder Viewing Room daily 7am–8.45pm

🚍 17, 29, 44

♿ Very good

💲 Free

❓ Free public tours Mar–Nov

Woodland Park Zoo

Woodland Park Zoo has won international recognition for its progressive design and is a highly respected leader in wildlife conservation.

Re-created habitats Most animals roam freely in their approximated "bioclimatic zones." The eight main exhibits—African Savanna (giraffes, hippos, lions), Australasia (wallabies, emus, snow leopards), Humboldt Penguin, Northern Trail (wolves, bears, eagles), Temperate Forest (red pandas, exotic birds), Trail of Adaptations (komodo dragons, meerkats, sloths), Tropical Asia (tigers, monkeys, orangutans, pythons) and Tropical Rain Forest (jaguars, lemurs, gorillas)—have won prestigious awards and introduce visitors not only to the animals, but also to corresponding plant species and ecosystems.

Take time out in the tranquil rose gardens at Woodland Park Zoo (top left); a jaguar cooling off in the water (bottom left); the giraffes (top right) and grizzly bears (bottom middle) are popular attractions; a plaque in the rose gardens dedicated to the efforts of the Lions Club and Seattle Rose Society (bottom right)

Other permanent exhibits include the Raptor Center with live flight demonstrations, the Family Farm with a petting zoo, and the seasonal Molbak's Butterfly Garden.

Tours and treats The zoo offers myriad tours, programs and activities for visitors young and old. Some of the most popular include keeper talks and feeding times, especially the jaguars and lions. For an additional fee, visitors can help feed some of the animals themselves, including birds and penguins.

For rainy days The zoo offers a special Rainy Day Building Hop map and it includes suggestions such as visiting the hand-carved carousel from 1918, which can be found in the zoo's North Meadow and costs $2/ride.

THE BASICS

zoo.org

➕ E2

✉ 5500 Phinney Avenue N

☎ 206/548-2500

🕐 May–Sep daily 9.30–6; Oct–Apr 9.30–4

🍴 Rain Forest Food Pavilion, Pacific Blue Chowder House

🚌 5

♿ Good

💲 Expensive; half price with purchase of CityPass; Off-peak tickets, Oct–Mar, are discounted.

❓ ZooTunes outdoor summer concerts on Wed nights, Jul–Aug; Wildlights festival Nov–Jan

More to See

BALLARD

A former maritime center with a distinctive Scandinavian flavor, Ballard has evolved into a bustling urban village that still retains an atmosphere of home-grown hospitality. The district is centered on Market Street and Ballard Avenue, with its beautifully restored 19th-century brick buildings. Some of the city's best restaurants, bars and craft breweries can be found in this neighborhood.

➕ Off map at A4 🚌 RapidRide D Line, 40, 61

BALLARD FARMERS MARKET

sfmamarkets.com
Opened in 2000, it has recently expanded and sells produce exclusively from Washington State farms, much of it organic. You'll also find prepared artisanal foods such as fresh bread, cheese and preserves. Food vendors serve up hot foods and musicians entertain the big crowds.

➕ Off map ✉ 22nd Avenue NW and NW Market Street 🕐 Sun 10–3

FISHERMEN'S TERMINAL

portseattle.org
Fishermen's Terminal is a great place to soak up the comings and goings of a large fleet. Fish have been an important local resource since Seattle's early days. In the early 1900s, a growing demand for salmon prompted the industry to lure new fishermen to the area—especially Scandinavian, Greek and Slavic immigrants. Since 1913, this has been the home base for the North Pacific fishing fleet. Washington fishers harvest 40 percent of all fish and other seafood caught in the United States. The *Fishermen's Memorial* dominates the Terminal's central plaza, a 30ft- (9m) high column, topped with a bronze sculpture of a fisherman, commemorates those who lost their lives at sea. There are eateries and shops at the terminal, so you can make a day of it.

➕ Off map at A5 ✉ 3919 18th Avenue W at Salmon Bay ☎ 206/787-3395 🕐 24 hours 🚌 29, 31 ♿ Very good ✋ Free

Fishing vessels gather in Fishermen's Terminal (left); the Fishermen's Memorial (right)

Shoppers hunting for a bargain at the Fremont Sunday market

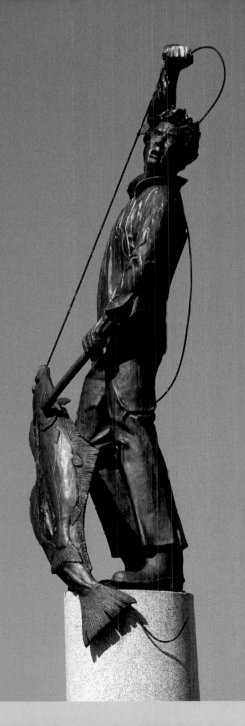

FREMONT SUNDAY MARKET

fremontmarket.com

Lively and large open-air European-style flea market with up to 200 vendors for visitors wishing to buy and browse antiques, collectibles, retro items, original and vintage fashion, jewelry, collectibles, crafts, flowers, and specialty foods. Street-food vendors and food trucks with every kind of cuisine are always on site and there's live music, too.

➕ B5 ✉ N 34th and Evanston Avenue N
🕐 Sun 10–4

GAS WORKS PARK

seattle.gov

This park on north Lake Union is popular for picnics, kite-flying, skate-boarding and wonderful views of Downtown. Rusted, graffiti-marked towers and brightly painted machinery in the play area recall this site's origins as a gas plant. Climb the grassy mound to see the park's sundial or launch a kite.

➕ E6 ✉ 2101 N Northlake Way
☎ 206/684-4075 🚌 26

NORDIC HERITAGE MUSEUM

nordicmuseum.org

This museum and cultural center is dedicated to honoring the legacy of Seattle's immigrants from the five Nordic countries: Denmark, Finland, Iceland, Norway and Sweden. Its modern, three-story building houses a collection of over 77,000 items, including fine art, furniture, textiles and boats.

➕ Off map ✉ 2655 NW Market Street
☎ 206/789-5707 🕐 Tue–Sat 10–4, Sun 12–4 🍴 Café 🚌 17, 29, 44 ♿ Great
🎟 Moderate; free 1st Thu of month
❓ Viking Days, Yulefest, workshops

WAITING FOR THE INTERURBAN

Richard Beyer's sculpture is a much-loved fixture of Fremont. Rarely are these gray aluminum trolley riders unadorned, either with scarves and hats in winter, or with balloons and banners to acknowl-edge someone's birthday.

➕ B6 ✉ Fremont Avenue N and N 34th Street 🚌 26, 28

Enjoy the eclectic mix of market wares at Fremont's weekly flea market

Shopping

LES AMIS

lesamis-inc.com

This rustic boutique is home to some fantastic frocks from the latest European and American designers.

🔲 Off map ✉ 3420 Evanston Avenue N ☎ 206/632-2877 🕐 Mon–Sat 11–6, Sun 11–5

ARTFX

artfx.net

More than 100 local artists and crafts-people from the Puget Sound region are represented by this gallery, which includes paintings, prints, sculpture, jewelry and more.

🔲 B5 ✉ 402 N 35th Street ☎ 206/545-7459 🕐 Thu–Sun 12–5

DANDELION BOTANICAL COMPANY

dandelionbotanical.com

Herbal apothecary with shelves stocked full of organic and ethically wildcrafted herbs, tinctures, essential oils, spices, salts and Chinese medicine

🔲 Off map ✉ 5424 Ballard Avenue NW ☎ 206/545-8892 🕐 Daily 10.30–7

FREMONT VINTAGE MALL

fremontvintagemall.com

Two floors full of 1940s–90s vintage art, collectibles, clothing, toys, furniture, housewares, records, and taxidermy. Occasionally you might find a good mid-century modern piece.

🔲 B5 ✉ 3419 Fremont Place N ☎ 206/329-4460 🕐 Mon–Sat 11–7, Sun 11–6

GOLD DOGS

shopgolddogs.com

Funky new and used clothing store for men and women. Known for their vintage cowboy boots and rock 'n' roll T-shirts.

🔲 B5 ✉ 5221 Ballard Avenue NW ☎ 206/499-1811 🕐 Mon–Thu 11–7.30, Fri–Sat 11–9, Sun 10–7.30

MONSTER ART, CLOTHING & GIFTS

monsterartandclothing.com

Ballard boutique featuring locally made and unusual art, crafts and clothing.

🔲 Off map ✉ 5000 20th Avenue NW ☎ 206/789-0037 🕐 Daily 10.30–6.30

PORTAGE BAY GOODS

portagebaygoods.com

Colorful and quirky environmentally friendly gifts, cards and stationery by local and worldwide artisans.

🔲 B6 ✉ 621 N 35th Street ☎ 206/547-5221 🕐 Daily 10–7

RE-SOUL

resoul.com

An eclectic blend of shoes, artwork, jewelry and home furnishings.

🔲 Off map ✉ 5319 Ballard Avenue NW ☎ 206/789-7312 🕐 Mon–Sat 11–8, Sun 11–5

SHOW PONY BOUTIQUE

showponyboutique.com

New and some used clothing and accessories for women, as well as gifts including candles, perfume and prints that are all mostly American-made and eco-friendly.

🔲 B5 ✉ 702 N 35th Street ☎ 206/706-4183 🕐 Mon–Sat 11–7, Sun 11–5

THEO CHOCOLATE

theochocolate.com

You can take a factory tour here, or just visit the shop for some of their delectable hard-crafted, organic, fair-trade confections.

🔲 35 ✉ 3400 Phinney Avenue N ☎ 206/632-5100 🕐 Daily 10–6

Where to Eat

PRICES	
Prices are approximate, based on a 3-course meal for one person.	
$$$	over $50
$$	$30–$50
$	under $30

CAFÉ BESALU ($)

cafebesalu.com

Delectable sweet and savory croissants, quiches, galettes, pretzels and lovely coffee. The pastries and ginger biscuits here are absolutely to die for.

➕ Off map ✉ 5909 24th Avenue NW
☎ 206/789-1463 🕐 6.30–4 (till 3 in fall and winter)

CAFÉ MUNIR ($$)

Worth the drive to the residential area of Ballard, this Lebanese restaurant serves up fresh, authentic, and mouth-watering mezze—small plates, including hummus, *mutabbal*, *fatayer* and *tabouleh*.

➕ Off map ✉ 2408 NW 80th Street
☎ 206/783-4190 🕐 Dinner Tue–Sun

CANLIS ($$$)

canlis.com

Fantastic views of Lake Union and beyond, white linens, top service. This is a special occasion kind of place where casual attire is frowned upon. The seasonal menu is Pacific Northwest with French accents.

➕ C7 ✉ 2576 Aurora Avenue N
☎ 206/283-3313 🕐 Dinner Mon–Sat

LA CARTA DE OAXACA ($$)

lacartadeoaxaca.com

One of Seattle's top Mexican restaurants with fantastic enchiladas. And try their signature *Tamale de Mole Negro* made with a chocolatey spicy sauce typical of the Oaxaca state.

➕ Off map ✉ 5431 Ballard Avenue NW
☎ 206/782-8722 🕐 Lunch Tue–Sat, dinner Mon–Sat

HATTIE'S HAT ($)

hatties-hat.com

A Seattle institution since who-knows-when, this joint is known for its classic American menu and its hand-carved bar.

➕ Off map ✉ 5231 Ballard Avenue NW
☎ 206/784-0175 🕐 Lunch and dinner daily, breakfast Sat, Sun

MANOLIN ($$)

manolinseattle.com

Pacific Northwest cuisine with an island flavor in a beachy setting, complete with a cozy patio. Cocktails are excellent. Come during their Happy Hour from 4–6 to beat the inevitable crowds.

➕ C5 ✉ 3621 Stone Way N ☎ 206/294-3331 🕐 Dinner Tue–Sun

PASEO CARIBBEAN FOOD ($)

paseorestaurants.com

The sandwiches at this casual spot are the best for miles around, especially the Caribbean Roast with slow-roasted and marinated pork on a lightly toasted baguette bun, topped with sweet and tasty caramelized onions.

➕ B4 ✉ 4225 Fremont Avenue N
☎ 206/545-7440 🕐 Lunch and dinner Tue–Sat, lunch only Sun

THE WALRUS AND THE CARPENTER ($$)

thewalrusbar.com

Busy and snug oyster bar with an open kitchen. Pretty salads and memorable desserts, too. If the line-up is long, have a drink next door at the Barnacle while you wait.

➕ Off map ✉ 4743 Ballard Avenue NW
☎ 206/395-9227 🕐 Dinner daily

FREMONT AND BALLARD WHERE TO EAT

96

Farther Afield

One of Seattle's greatest attributes is its proximity to towering mountains, sparkling waterways and forests. The region is also blessed with picturesque rural towns and ideal day-trip destinations.

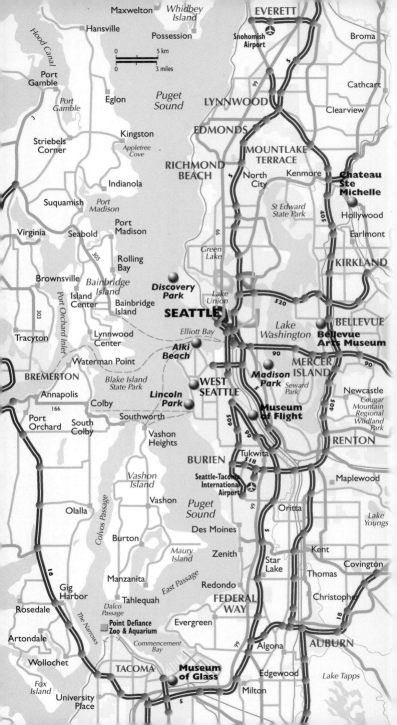

Farther Afield

Alki Beach and West Seattle

HIGHLIGHTS

- Pickup games of beach volleyball
- Driftwood beach fires at sunset
- People-watching on the crowded promenade
- Amazing views of Downtown

TIP

- There's limited street parking at the beach. The water taxi from Downtown to West Seattle is a good (and scenic) alternative.

Alki Beach is Seattle's birthplace. Today, its sandy shore and waterfront trail are busy in the summer months with city folk looking to relax.

Beginnings The Duwamish and Suquamish peoples were on hand to meet the schooner *Exact* when it sailed into Elliott Bay on November 13, 1851. The ship anchored off Alki Point and Arthur Denny and his party of 23 paddled their skiff ashore. The locals proved friendly and the Denny party decided to stay. They set about building four log cabins, wistfully naming their new home New York–Alki, "Alki" being a word in the Chinook language for "someday," an indication of Denny's ambitions. The following year, after surviving fierce winter storms, the settlers decided to move across

The whitewashed Alki Point Lighthouse safeguards against any dangers on Puget Sound (left, bottom right); children paddling in the waters of Puget Sound off Alki Beach (top middle); the beautiful sandy shoreline (bottom middle); the grassy areas stretching alongside Alki Beach are popular with picnickers (top right)

Elliott Bay to the more sheltered, deepwater harbor that is today's Pioneer Square.

Beach life The beach itself is the main attraction today. Enjoy the views, fine sand, a paved trail, and boat and bike rentals. There's food and drink, too—try Phoenecia (for pizza), Spud Fish & Chips, or the Pepperdock Restaurant (for ice cream). You can walk, bike or skate the 2.5 miles (4km) from Alki Beach to Duwamish Head. Continue south along the water to lovely Lincoln Park for the outdoor pool and waterslide.

Scuba in Seattle Alki Beach is a popular destination for Seattle's diehard divers. Most dive at the eastern end of the beach, not far from Salty's restaurant. The water temperature ranges from 46 to 56°F (8 to 14°C).

THE BASICS

See map ▷ 98

3201 Alki Avenue SW (Alki Point Lighthouse)

206/684-4075

Lighthouse Sat–Sun 1–4. Coast Guard officer on duty Jun–Aug

37, 50, 56,

King County West Seattle Water Taxi from Pier 50 Downtown (Mon–Sat, Mon–Fri in winter)

Bike, paddleboard and boat rentals; driftwood fires permitted on beach

Discovery Park

Miles of beach stretch around the edge of the park, overlooking Puget Sound

THE BASICS

Discovery Park
seattle.gov/parks
⊞ See map ▷ 98
✉ 3801 W Government Way
☎ 206/386-4236
🕐 Park: daily dawn to dusk. Visitor center: daily 8.30–5 (except national holidays)
🚌 24, 33
♿ Poor
✋ Free

Daybreak Star Arts Center
☎ 206/285-4425
🕐 Mon–Fri 9–5
♿ Very good
❓ Salmon lunch/Artmart, Sat in Dec; Seafair Indian Pow-Wow Days, 3rd weekend in Jul

DID YOU KNOW?

● Area: 534 acres (216ha).
● Bald eagles sometimes nest in the park.
● During World War II, the area was a major induction and training center for troops.

TIP

● If you're short on time but still want a good view of Puget Sound, park at the South Beach lot. From there, it's a short walk to the majestic West Point Light Station, a lighthouse built in 1881.

This park is the largest area of wilderness in the city. Its meadows, forests, cliffs, marshes and shoreline provide habitat for a host of different birds and animals.

Legacy of the military The 534 forested acres (216ha) on Magnolia Bluff that is Discovery Park was a military base from the 1890s, but in 1970 the government turned it over to the city for use as a park. During the transfer, an alliance of local tribes petitioned to regain ancestral land they felt was theirs, and 20 acres (8ha) were set aside for a Native American cultural center.

Discover the trails The park's great size means that there are miles of nature and bike trails to be explored. Test your fitness along the half-mile "parcours" (health path) through the woods. To the west, 2 miles (3km) of beach extend north and south from the West Point lighthouse (head south for sand, north for rocks). To get to the beach, pick up the loop trail at the north or south parking lot. The park's visitor center provides free 90-minute walks led by a naturalist, every Saturday at 2pm.

Daybreak Star Arts Center The structure uses enormous cedar timbers to reflect the points of a star. Native American art adorns the walls inside—the Arts Center is one of only four dedicated to contemporary Native American work in the United States. Highlights of the collection include *The Earth is Our Mother* by Jimmie C. Fife and paintings by Robert Montoya.

Museum of Flight

Two of the many exhibits proudly presented at the Museum of Flight

This stunning building is not only one of the largest, but also one of the finest air and space museums in the world.

Red Barn and Airpark This is where Boeing's first planes were built, and displays cover the company's history and early days of flight. You'll meet the Wright brothers and see a model of their 1903 Flyer. Outside, in the Airpark, you can visit six of the largest aircraft, including the first jet Air Force One and a Concorde.

Great Gallery and Space Gallery The airy and breathtaking Great Gallery traces the story of flight from early mythology to the latest accomplishments in space. Overhead, more than 20 full-size airplanes hang at varying levels from a ceiling grid. All face the same direction, like a squadron frozen in flight. Altogether there are more than 150 iconic air and space craft on display. Another exhibit contains objects from the Apollo space program, including an Apollo command module, Apollo 12 and 16 F-1 engines, lunar rocks and the Lunar Roving Vehicle. You can also see the NASA Space Shuttle Trainer in which every Shuttle astronaut honed their skills.

Control the traffic Using the latest technology, the Flight Tower simulates the work of air traffic controllers and their communications with pilots, but it gets real too. You can view the King County International Airport and hear live communications with incoming flights.

THE BASICS

museumofflight.org

📍 See map ▷ 98

✉ 9404 E Marginal Way S by Boeing Field

☎ 206/764-5720

🕐 Daily 10–5 (1st Thu of month until 9)

🍴 Wings Café and Pavilion Café

🚌 124

♿ Excellent

💲 Expensive. Free 1st Thu of month, 5–9pm

❓ Family workshops; special events

HIGHLIGHTS

● A restored 1917 Curtiss "Jenny" biplane
● A flying replica of the B&W, Boeing's first plane
● The only M-21 Blackbird spy plane in existence
● Apollo space program objects
● A full-size air traffic control tower
● Piloting an imaginary flight
● NASA Space Shuttle Trainer

FARTHER AFIELD TOP 25

More to See

BELLEVUE ARTS MUSEUM (BAM)

bellevuearts.org

Across Lake Washington on Seattle's Eastside, BAM shows contemporary visual art, craft and design of the Northwest. The building's sculptural qualities and architect Stephen Holl's use of natural light have created a luminous space that both explores and generates art.

➕ See map ▷ 98　✉ 510 Bellevue Way NE　☎ 425/519-0770　🕐 Wed–Sun 11–5 (1st Fri until 8)　🚌 550 from bus tunnel　💲 Moderate; free 1st Fri of month

CHATEAU STE. MICHELLE

ste-michelle.com

Washington's award-winning and oldest winery, producing Chardonnay, Cabernet, Merlot and Riesling. Tour and tastings are complimentary and are held daily from 10–5.

➕ See map ▷ 98　✉ 14111 NE 145th Street in Woodinville, NE of Seattle　☎ 425/488-1133　🚌 255 to Kirkland, then 236 to Woodville　💲 Free; premium and vintage wine tastings available for a fee

FUTURE OF FLIGHT AVIATION CENTER AND BOEING TOUR

futureofflight.org

Over the years, Seattle's fortunes have soared and dipped on the wings of Boeing. Take a 90-minute tour of this magnificent factory and discover what lies ahead.

➕ See map ▷ 98　✉ 8415 Paine Field Boulevard, Mukilteo　☎ 800/464-1476　🚌 512 to Everett, then 113 to Mukilteo (it's a half-mile walk from the stop)　🕐 Future of Flight Center: daily 8.30–5.30; tours 9–3 on the hour; height restriction on tour for children under 4ft (122cm)　💲 Expensive

LINCOLN PARK

seattle.gov

A lovely West Seattle park south of Alki with something for everyone: great views, rocky beaches with tidepools, walking and biking trails, tennis courts and a saltwater pool.

➕ See map ▷ 98　✉ Fauntleroy Avenue SW and SW Webster　☎ 206/684-4075　🚌 54

MADISON PARK

seattle.gov

In this neighborhood beach park, on the western shore of Lake Washington, you can sunbathe on the grassy slope. There's also a bathhouse and a swimming dock with a diving board. Lifeguards operate throughout the summer.

➕ See map ▷ 98　✉ The foot of E Madison Street at 43rd Avenue E　🚌 11　☎ 206/684-4075　🕐 Daily dawn–dusk

MUSEUM OF GLASS

museumofglass.org

South of Seattle lies Tacoma, home of glass artist Dale Chihuly (▷ 48), where this dazzling Museum of Glass occupies 13,000sq ft (3,963sq m) of exhibition space. The glass-walled structure incorporates in its design a 90ft (27m) steel cone housing the Hot Shop, where you can watch glassworkers shape enormous molten globs into art. A dramatic glass bridge connects the museum to the Washington State History Museum.

➕ See map ▷ 98　✉ 1801 Dock Street, Tacoma　☎ 253/284-4719　🕐 Late May–early Sep Mon–Sat 10–5, Sun 12–5; early Sep–late May Wed–Sat 10–5, Sun 12–5 (3rd Thu 10–8)　🍴 Choripan　🚂 Sounder train　🚌 Sound Transit #594　💲 Moderate

Excursions

HURRICANE RIDGE/ OLYMPIC NATIONAL PARK

nps.gov

Olympic National Park is one of the nation's most diverse parks; its boundaries encompass remote ocean beaches, primeval temperate rain forests, and high alpine glaciers and ridgelines. Hurricane Ridge rises nearly a vertical mile above Port Angeles and the northern end of the Olympic Peninsula. When the sun emerges, the Ridge's visitors enjoy endless views of the Strait of Juan de Fuca, Vancouver Island and beyond.

A visitor center greets you at the summit and a series of nature trails provide ample opportunities for hiking and enjoying the park's natural flora and fauna. Sure, the drive from Seattle s sign ficant, but the variety of wild spaces you'll encounter make the trip well worth it. Don't forget your raincoat, though. During the winter months, skiing and snowboarding is possible, but the road is only open Friday through Sunday, weather permitting.

THE BASICS

Distance: 100 miles (160km) northwest of Seattle
Journey Time: 3 hours by road and Washington State Ferry
Route: I-5 north to Edmonds; take the ferry to Kingston; west on 104 to 101; north on 101 to Port Angeles; south on Hurricane Ridge Road to visitor center
Bus Tours: Cloberouter (408/904/3068); Evergreen Escapes (866/203-7603)
Olympic National Park: ☎ 360/565-3130
Hurricane Ridge Visitor Center: ☎ 360/565-3131

MOUNT RAINIER

nps.gov

Mount Rainier, one of a string of active volcanoes running south from the Canadian border to California, rises 14,410ft (4,392m) above sea level, and the upper 6,000ft (1,800m) are covered in snow year-round.

On clear days, the mountain's white dome, apparently hovering over Seattle, has an appearance so immediate that it's hard to believe it's actually 90 miles (145km) away. Small wonder that native peoples ascribed supernatural power to the mountain. For a closer view of Mount Rainier's peak, drive to Crystal Mountain and take the gondola to its summit. For information on hiking, stop at Longmire, then drive on for 11 miles (18km) to the Henry M. Jackson Memorial Visitor Center at Paradise, where many of the trails begin. The 93-mile (150-km) Wonderland Trail, built in 1915, circumnavigates Mount Rainer and takes up to two weeks to complete on foot.

THE BASICS

Distance: 90 miles (145km) southeast of Seattle
Journey Time: 2.5 hours by road
Route: I-5 south to Tacoma; east on route 512; south on route 7 and east on route 706 to the park entrance
Bus Tours: Tours Northwest ☎ 888/293-1404; Discover Nature ☎ 253/777-8226
Mt. Rainier National Park: ☎ 360/569-2211
Henry M. Jackson Memorial Visitor Center at Paradise: ☎ 360/569-6571

FARTHER AFIELD EXCURSIONS

THE BASICS

Journey Time: 2.5–3 hours by boat

🚢 Victoria Clipper, Pier 69 ☎ 206/448-500 or 800/888-2535; clippervacations.com

🕐 Enquire for schedule

❓ A visit to Victoria means crossing the border into Canada, so you'll need to take your passport and other necessary travel documents

VICTORIA, BRITISH COLUMBIA

British Columbia's capital city is a verdant paradise complete with year-round flowers, gorgeous architecture and a historical downtown seaport.

With its many festivals and holiday celebrations, the city honors its cultural influences, both British and Native. High-speed catamarans cruise Puget Sound and the Strait of Juan de Fuca, and sail into Victoria, Canada, for a taste of England (with formal gardens, double-decker buses and shops selling tweeds and Irish linen). At the Royal British Columbia Museum you can view items made by First Americans living on the Northwest Coast. Visit Craigdarroch Castle, an elegant and haunted turreted mansion from 1890, to view period furnishings and beautiful stained-glass windows. Take a bus to the delightful Butchart Gardens or take tea in the imperial splendor of the Empress Hotel.

THE BASICS

Distance: 30 miles (48km) northwest of Seattle

Journey Time: 1.5 hours by road and Washington State Ferry

Route: I–5 north to Mukilteo; take ferry to Clinton; west on 525 to Langley, Freeland and Coupeville

Langley: ☎ 360/221-6765; visitlangley.com

Coupeville: ☎ 360/678-5434; cometocoupeville.com

Ebey's Landing:
☎ 360/678-6084; nps.gov

WHIDBEY ISLAND

Lying 30 miles (50km) northwest of Seattle, Whidbey Island is a welcome counterpoint to the city's hustle and bustle and is a popular retreat for city dwellers.

Dotted with farms, lush forests, small towns, country roads and sandy beaches, the island has an active, vibrant community of its own. Whidbey is approximately 60 miles (100km) long, and in many places it's less than 2 miles (3km) in width.

The north end of the island is dominated by a naval base and the associated city of Oak Harbor, but the south end is far more scenic. Of particular note are the communities of Langley and Coupeville, both of which have historic downtowns, excellent restaurants and shopping, and top-flight bed-and-breakfast inns. Ebey's Landing National Historical Reserve is one of the Puget Sound's most beautiful waterfront parks, and it shouldn't be passed over. Deception Pass State Park, too, is breathtaking with its high bridge from the 1930s, large whirlpools and secluded coves.

You're bound to find the perfect place to rest your head in this city, where lodgings range from historic bed-and-breakfasts to modern penthouse suites. Many hotels Downtown even throw in a great view of Puget Sound, as well.

Where to Stay

Introduction

Seattle is home to a wide range of lodging choices, including luxury boutique hotels, major chains, bed-and-breakfasts and everything in between.

Budget or Luxury?

There are a number of inexpensive chain hotels in the city, as well as more than a few independent budget properties and a smattering of B&Bs. There are several hotels competing for high-end visitors and most pull out all the stops to impress their guests. These hotels are centered around the Downtown area and rarely disappoint.

Where to Stay

The majority of the city's hotels are in and around Downtown, but accommodations can be found in all outlying neighborhoods. The bustling University District is not a bad place to stay, considering the proximity to the city, and the hotels here are less expensive than those Downtown. Although the waterfront is a tourist hot spot, it is not the easiest place to find a hotel. Bordering the eastern edge of Lake Union, Eastlake offers moderately priced, large residence-style hotels, and is still convenient for the city. Bellevue and the Eastside, across Lake Washington, are ideal spots for visitors who don't mind a short commute; the lodgings here range in quality and price and are convenient to business and shopping. If you prefer not to stray far from Sea-Tac Airport (about half an hour from Downtown), there are plenty of options—if you don't mind the plane noise.

PERKS AND PARKING

● Most accommodations in Seattle offer complimentary WiFi, some include a hearty breakfast, but few provide free parking. Expect to pay an often hefty fee for your vehicle.

● Bed-and-breakfast accommodations will often have free parking available, though it is usually of the on-street variety so check the signage for limitations. Sundays and holidays are free street parking days in Seattle.

Comfort and style awaits the weary traveller, whatever your budget

Budget Hotels

PRICES

Expect to pay under $150 for a double room per night in a budget hotel.

BED & BREAKFAST INN

seattlebednbreakfast.com

Perks at this Capitol Hill B&B include off-street parking, free WiFi and a generous breakfast buffet with organic local ingredients. Most rooms have shared bathrooms, so ask for the Mini Ensuite room if you prefer a private bathroom all to yourself.

➕ H12 ✉ 1808 E Denny Way ☎ 206/412-7378 (10–6 only) or 206/323-1955 🚌 8, 12

THE GATEWOOD BED & BREAKFAST

gatewoodwestseattle.com

Spotless, modern rooms with hardwood floors, private bathrooms, micro-fiber bedding, Turkish cotton towels and free WiFi in a restored 1910 home in West Seattle. The breakfast is ample and delicious and there's parking on site. The quiet neighborhood is lovely for strolling, and there are restaurants, shops and the beach all within a mile's walk (1.6km) away.

➕ Off map ✉ 7446 Gatewood Rd SW ☎ 206/938-3482 🚌 22

GEORGETOWN INN

georgetowninnseattle.com

Located in an industrial, up-and-coming neighborhood south of Downtown, all the basic but clean rooms have private bathrooms, fridges, and good-quality toiletries. Some rooms have kitchenettes. The parking, WiFi continental breakfast and lobby treats are all complimentary

➕ Off map ✉ 6100 Corson Avenue S ☎ 206/762-2233 🚌 60, 124

MOORE HOTEL

moorehotel.com

Built in 1907, this Downtown hotel is also home to the famous Moore Theatre. The hotel rooms are simple, some have private bathrooms and kitchenettes. There is an elevator, and discounted parking for guests. The Moore Coffee Shop downstairs has stellar coffee, waffles and sandwiches.

➕ D14 ✉ 1926 2nd Avenue ☎ 206/448-4851 🚌 10, 12, 15, 13

PANAMA HOTEL

panamahotel.net

Vintage furnishings, shared bathrooms, and clean comfortable beds in a historic 1910 hotel in Chinatown. The Tea & Coffee House (▷ 44) downstairs is lovely and there are great eateries within easy walking distance. Note that there are no elevators available and rooms are up two flights of stairs.

➕ F16 ✉ 605 S Main Street ☎ 206/223-9242 🚈 Light Rail 5th & Jackson Station; Bus: 1, 7, 14, 36, 49

UNIVERSITY MOTEL SUITES

universitymotelsuites.com

Large suites on a quiet street in the University district. Each unit has separate bedrooms with kitchen. Plain furnishings, but good space and free parking.

➕ G4 ✉ 4731 12th Avenue ☎ 206/522-4724 🚌 45, 67, 71, 73, 74

B&B ASSOCIATION

The Seattle Bed & Breakfast Association represents independently owned, inspected B&Bs and inns, with members in and around Seattle, but all within 30 minutes of the airport. Their website has information and links to member websites.

☎ 206/547-1020; lodginginseattle.com

Mid-Range Hotels

11TH AVENUE INN

11thavenueinn.com

Charming B&B in Capitol Hill, within easy walking distance to sites, shops and restaurants. Rooms have private bathrooms, WiFi, vintage furniture and hardwood floors. Breakfast and parking on site is included. For a little more privacy you can ask for the Barn 11—a renovated little barn at the back.

G16 121 11th Avenue E 206/720-7161 8, 10, 43; Light Rail Capitol Hill Station

ACE HOTEL

acehotel.com

Small but stylish rooms with original artwork, mini-bars and large windows, some with partial water views. Some rooms have private bathrooms, others share bathrooms down the hall. Continental breakfast is included and the lively Belltown location is hard to beat.

C13 2423 1st Avenue 206/448-4721

BACON MANSION

baconmansion.com

Elegant B&B in Capitol Hill in an Edwardian-style Tudor home from 1909. Rooms are richly decorated, some have private bathrooms, fireplaces and kitchenettes. Continental breakfast provided.

G14 959 Broadway E 206/329-1864 25, 49

BELLTOWN INN

belltown-inn.com

Central location, colourful, funky decor, and all the rooms include kitchenettes, windows that open and air conditioning. The concierge offers free bike rentals, and the rooftop sun deck is lovely for an evening drink with a view.

C13 2301 3rd Avenue 206/529-3700 1, 2, 3, 4, 5, 13

GASLIGHT INN

gaslight-inn.com

Restored Arts and Crafts mansion in Capitol Hill with cozy rooms, some of which feature private bathrooms, air conditioning, fireplaces, and balconies with views. Continental breakfast is provided and the lovely courtyard has a heated pool and koi pond.

H13 1727 15th Avenue 206/325-3654 8, 10, 11

HOTEL FIVE

staypineapple.com/hotel-five-seattle-wa

Just a few blocks from Pike Place Market, this funky, pet-friendly hotel in Belltown has colorful, modern rooms featuring hardwood floors, rain showers and Keurig coffee makers in the rooms. Perks include afternoon cupcakes, bicycles to borrow, on site fitness center and a free shuttle service to nearby sites. The hotel also has a parking garage (fee applies).

D13 2200 Fifth Avenue 206/441-9785 27, 37, 62

LODGING GUIDES

● The Seattle tourist organization's website, visitseattle.org, includes a hotel guide and the Hotel Concierge booking service, offering deals and discounts.
● The Pacific Reservation Service has a website at seattlebedandbreakfast.com. Click on "Find the Perfect Place" and then select from a list of options to find appealing lodgings in residential areas.

HOTEL MAX

hotelmaxseattle.com

Swanky, ultramodern hotel featuring more than 350 pieces of original art by local artists. Rooms have thick pillowtop mattresses, plush robes, gourmet coffees and teas, private bars and a menu from which to select your pillows.

✚ D13 ✉ 620 Stewart Street ☎ 206/728-6299 or 366/833-6299 🛏 1, 2, 4, 5 and many others

HYATT PLACE SEATTLE/ DOWNTOWN

hyattplace.com

Modern family-friendly hotel just a few blocks from Seattle Center. Most of the spacious rooms have views of the city. Perks include free WiFi, a hot breakfast, and a shuttle service. There's an on site gym and indoor pool as well.

✚ C12 ✉ 110 6th Avenue N ☎ 206/441-6041 🛏 8

KIMPTON HOTEL VINTAGE

hotelvintage-seattle.com

A lovely Downtown boutique hotel with a wine-themed decor. Each room is dedicated to a local winery or vineyard. Amenities galore, including 24-hour room service, a nightly wine reception in the lobby, soundproof windows and a yoga mat in every room.

✚ E15 ✉ 1100 5th Avenue ☎ 206/624-8000 🛏 2, 13

MARQUEEN HOTEL

marqueen.com

Classic brick building from 1918 with large, apartment-like vintage rooms that have hardwood floors and antique furnishings. Continental breakfast is included.

✚ B11 ✉ 600 Queen Anne Avenue N ☎ 206/282-7407 🛏 1, 8, 32

MAYFLOWER PARK HOTEL

mayflowerpark.com

Locally owned and independent Downtown hotel, built in 1927, with comfortable and clean rooms, with complimentary WiFi, mini-fridges and coffee makers. The jazz and cocktail bar by the lobby is a classic, and the Andaluca Restaurant does weekend brunch.

✚ D14 ✉ 405 Olive Way ☎ 206/623-8700 or 800/426-5100

THE MEDITERRANEAN INN

mediterranean-inn.com

Apartment-like rooms at this Queen Anne neighborhood hotel, with kitchenettes, windows that open, air conditioning and free WiFi. There's also a gym and a Starbucks, and free bicycle rentals. The best part is the rooftop deck with fantastic water and city views.

✚ A11 ✉ 425 Queen Anne Avenue N ☎ 206/428-4700 🛏 1, 2, 8, 13, 29

SILVER CLOUD INN–LAKE UNION

silvercloud.com

Most rooms have waterfront views of Lake Union, plus all have free WiFi, microwaves, coffee makers, and fridges. Breakfast is included. There's an indoor pool, gym, and free shuttle service.

✚ E10 ✉ 1150 Fairview Avenue N ☎ 206/447-9500 or 800/330-5812

WATERTOWN HOTEL

watertownseattle.com

Just four blocks away from the University of Washington, this friendly hotel has modern rooms with hardwood floors, free WiFi, and in-room Keurig coffee makers. There's also a fitness center and café on site. Complimentary bicycles and shuttle bus into central Seattle.

✚ G3 ✉ 4242 Roosevelt Way NE ☎ 206/826-4242 🛏 65, 67, 74

Luxury Hotels

ALEXIS HOTEL

alexishotel.com

Chic and modern meets luxury vintage at this Downtown boutique hotel. The sumptuous rooms include goose-down comforters, Amazon Echo Dots (your own personal concierge device), and mini-bars filled with tempting local treats. In addition there are nightly wine and morning coffee and tea receptions.

➕ D15 ✉ 1007 1st Avenue ☎ 206/624-4844

FAIRMONT OLYMPIC HOTEL

fairmont.com

Grand and elegant 1924 Downtown hotel with family-friendly features including an indoor pool, child-sized bathrobes and toiletry kits, and a children's dining menu. The modern, air-conditioned rooms are spacious and have marble en-suite bathrooms, Keurig coffee makers and down bedding.

➕ E15 ✉ 411 University Street ☎ 206/621-1700

FOUR SEASONS

fourseasons.com

With a central Downtown location, this contemporary high-rise hotel has spacious, light-filled rooms from the floor-to-ceiling windows. There's a fine dining restaurant, rooftop pool and a chic spa.

➕ D5 ✉ 99 Union Street ☎ 206/749-7000
🚇 Central Link to University Street

HOTEL ANDRA

hotelandra.com

Scandinavian-style luxury in Belltown, with bright, modern rooms that feature large windows, feather pillows and spa-like bathrooms. The hotel restaurant, Lola, has a fantastic Greek menu and is excellent for brunch as well.

➕ D14 ✉ 2000 4th Avenue ☎ 206/448-860

HOTEL SORRENTO

hotelsorrento.com

Built in 1909, this landmark hotel's first guest was US President William Taft. Situated on the top of First Hill, the elegant rooms have original features, period furnishings and white marble bathrooms. The Fireside Room is a local treasure.

➕ F15 ✉ 900 Madison Street ☎ 206/622-6400

INN AT THE MARKET

innatthemarket.com

Located right at Pike Place Market, the views are hard to beat at this ultra-indulgent hotel. Sophisticated rooms are fitted with top-end furnishings and amenities, while the four on site restaurants are some of the best in the city. The rooftop deck is fabulous, too. For your ultimate home-away-from-home, ask for the Beecher's Loft suite.

➕ D14 ✉ 86 Pine Street ☎ 206/443-3600 or 800/446-4484

PAN PACIFIC SEATTLE

panpacific.com

This classic, large, pet-friendly hotel is situated Downtown, and has contemporary rooms with spacious bathrooms, floor-to-ceiling windows with views, and Egyptian cotton bed linens. Added touches are the Herman Miller chairs, the well-equipped fitness center and the complimentary car service within a two-mile (3.2km) radius of the hotel.

➕ D12 ✉ 2125 Terry Avenue ☎ 206/264-8111 or 877/324-4856

The following section will help you plan your visit to Seattle. We have suggested the best ways to get around the city and provided useful information for while you are there.

Need to Know

Planning Ahead

When to Go

Seattle is a year-round destination and focal point for arts in the Pacific Northwest. Ringed by ski resorts, Seattle attracts winter sports enthusiasts, and sports fans visit during the baseball and football seasons. Hotel reservations are a must at any time of year.

TIME

Seattle is on Pacific Standard Time, three hours behind New York, eight hours behind the UK.

AVERAGE DAILY MAXIMUM TEMPERATURES

JAN	FEB	MAR	APR	MAY	JUN	JUL	AUG	SEP	OCT	NOV	DEC
45°F	50°F	53°F	59°F	66°F	70°F	76°F	75°F	69°F	62°F	51°F	47°F
7°C	10°C	12°C	13°C	19°C	21°C	24°C	24°C	20°C	16°C	10°C	8°C

Spring (March to May) brings a flurry of bulbs and flowering trees; weather can be unsettled.

Summer (June to August) is sunny and clear, with cool nights. Plan to dress in layers.

Fall (September to November) is often lovely, particularly September, with rainfall averaging 1.8in (5cm).

Winter (December to February) rarely brings snow to the city, although the Cascade and Olympic mountains receive vast quantities. November to January are the rainiest months.

WHAT'S ON

January/February Chinese and Vietnamese New Year's Celebration; Seattle Boat Show.

February Seattle Museum Month: Downtown hotel guests get half-price tickets.

February/March Fat Tuesday: Mardi Gras celebrations across the city.

March Moisture Festival; Taste Washington: Wine and food festival.

April Arcade Lights Artisan Food, Craft Beer and Wine Festival at Pike Place Market; Cherry Blossom and Japanese Cultural Festival;

Seattle Restaurant Week.

May Opening Day of Boating Season (first Saturday); Seattle Maritime Festival; University District Street Fair; Northwest Folklife Festival; Seattle International Film Festival.

June Fremont Fair: longest day celebrations; Seattle Pride.

July 4 July; Out to Lunch Summer: Downtown concerts; Olympic Music Festival; Lake Union Wooden Boat Festival; Chinatown-International District Dragon Fest; Bite

of Seattle Food Fest.

August Seafair: Races on water with milk-carton derbies and hydrofoil heats. Chief Seattle Days: powwow; Viking Days: weekend of re-enactments, crafts and food in Ballard.

September Bumbershoot: Festival of music, visual arts and crafts.

October–November Seattle Children's Festival; Earshot Jazz Festival.

December Christmas Ships: Brightly-lit vessels visit the beaches with caroling choirs.

Seattle Online

visitseattle.org
The Seattle–King County Visitors Bureau website. Listings and a calendar of events.

seattle.eater.com and thrillist.com/seattle
Both sites have comprehensive info on Seattle's restaurants, bars and nightlife, written by experienced locals. Find out about the newest openings, festivals and attractions, too.

seattlemet.com
Pacific Northwest arts and entertainment guide, service of a local media company, with links to hotels, tours, transportation, shopping, restaurants and the outdoors.

tripplanner.kingcounty.gov
Helps you plan bus transportation from points A to B. Provides route numbers, stop locations, schedules and next-bus-out information.

wsdot.wa.gov/ferries
Official Washington State ferry website, with schedule and fare information.

oyster.com
Excellent hotel guide with unedited hotel photos, professional reviews and recommendations. Includes last-minute deals and online reservations.

weather.com
Weather information by city and zip code; current conditions, 10-day forecast, weather alerts and satellite photographs.

Amtrak.com
Route, fare and schedule information and online booking for Amtrak rail service.

seattletimes.com
The city's main daily newspaper with up-to-the-minute local and regional news, plus a reliable entertainment and restaurant review section.

TRAVEL SITES

fodors.com
A complete travel-planning site. Research prices and weather; book air tickets, cars and rooms.

seattle.gov
A wide range of information for visitors includes the current week's events, large and small.

experiencewa.com
Everything you need to know to venture farther afield.

STAYING CONNECTED

Free WiFi is available all over the city. Starbucks and other coffee shops are prime spots, though you'll be expected to buy something. You can also get online at the Seattle Center, and in all of the city's public libraries. If you don't have a laptop or smartphone, the central library has computers for public use, available for 30 minutes with a guest pass or for longer if you buy a library card. Some businesses have open access too, and specific locations are listed on openwifispots. com, which enables you to search by neighborhood or category (bookstores, shopping malls, gas stations, etc).

Getting There

ENTRY REQUIREMENTS

International travelers going to the US under the Visa Waiver Program (VWP) are now subject to enhanced security requirements. Online completion and approval of ESTA (Electronic System for Travel Authorization), along with payment of the fee, is mandatory ahead of travel for all VWP travelers. For full details, go to the official website esta.cbp.dhs.gov.

CUSTOMS REGULATIONS

Duty-free allowances include 1 liter of alcoholic spirits or wine (no one under 21 may bring in alcohol), 200 cigarettes and 100 cigars (not Cuban) and up to $100-worth of gifts. Some medications may be prescription-only in the US and may be confiscated. Bring a doctor's certificate for essential medication.

AIRPORT

Sea-Tac International Airport is 13 miles (20km) south of Downtown Seattle. Flights from New York take 5–6 hours, from LA 2–3 hours and from London about 10 hours. Upon arrival, look for the large airport maps near the escalators.

30 miles (48km)   20 miles (32km)   10 miles (16km)   • Seattle

⊠ Sea-Tac International Airport

FROM SEA-TAC INTERNATIONAL AIRPORT

For airport information call 206/787-5388 and there's an information desk near Baggage Claim. There are a variety of ways to make your way from the airport to Downtown Seattle. Travel time is 20 minutes or more, depending on your choice of transportation mode and traffic conditions.

The Link Light Rail service runs Mon–Sat 5am–1am, Sun 6am–midnight, with trains every 6–15 minutes, depending on the time of day. It will get you to downtown Seattle in about 30 minutes and costs around $3.

The Downtown Airporter bus (tel 855/566-3300) departs twice an hour (6.30am–9pm) from the inner drive curb on the 3rd floor of the Airport Garage, with service to and from major hotels; cost is about $18.

King County Metro Transit buses leave from bus stops on International Boulevard (State Highway 99) and South 176th Street near the Link Light Rail Station; exact change is required and the ticket costs between $2.25 and $3 one-way (tel 206/553-3000 or log on to the website, tripplanner.kingcounty.gov).

Taxis, ride-sharing companies (Uber, Lyft), and limousines pick up passengers on the third floor of the parking garage, across from the Main Terminal. Limousines also pick up at the curb outside Baggage Claim. Fares are between $40–$55 to Downtown. Thirteen rental companies occupy the Rental Car Facility, reached by a 24-hour shuttle bus from Baggage Claim.

ARRIVING BY BUS
Greyhound (tel 800/231-2222) buses arrive and leave from Seattle's Greyhound Terminal Downtown at 503 S Royal Brougham Way.

ARRIVING BY CAR
If you arrive by car you will enter the city via I–5. Downtown exits are Union Street (for City Center) and James Street (for Pioneer Square). If arriving via I–90 from the east you will cross the Homer M. Hadley Memorial Bridge; from there follow signs to I–5 north for Downtown exits. If you intend to rent a car and are not a US citizen, bring your foreign license and an international driver's license, which must be acquired before arriving. Most car rental agencies require a major credit card; many will not rent a car to persons under 25.

ARRIVING BY TRAIN
Amtrak trains (tel 206/624-0618) arrive at King Street Station at 3rd and Jackson, between Pioneer Square and the International District. The journey from LA takes 35 hours. From New York, change trains in Chicago (NY–Chicago 18–21 hours, Chicago–Seattle 47 hours).

DRIVING IN SEATTLE

Slow-moving traffic and even gridlock is common on Interstate 5, Seattle's only North–South freeway. Avenues and streets may have either names or numbers, but virtually all have helpful directional designations (NE, SW). Downtown Seattle has both on-street metered parking and garages and lots. Most meters cost $2–$3 per hour, with a two-hour limit—and meter attendants are vigilant. Unlimited free parking on Sundays and some holidays.

VISITORS WITH DISABILITIES

Downtown Seattle streets, especially those running east to west, can be difficult for travelers with a disability because of the city's steep hills. Streets and public buildings are required to have ramps, and some neighborhoods are level and evenly paved. All of the city's buses have wheelchair lifts and designated space on the bus. For more information check the websites for Mobility International USA (miusa.org).

Getting Around

NEED TO KNOW   GETTING AROUND

SAFETY

● Exercise caution and at night avoid the areas around 1st to 2nd and Pike, the edges of Pioneer Square, Northgate between 3rd and 5th, and most of all the area between 2nd and 4th from James to Yesler.
● Seattle police are well known for giving out tickets to jaywalkers.

ORGANIZED TOURS

● Bill Speidel's Underground Tour: See Seattle's subterranean storefronts and sidewalks from pre-1889. (☎ 206/682-4646; undergroundtour.com)
● Seattle Seaplanes: get a bird's-eye view of the city (☎ 206/329-9638; seattleseaplanes.com)
● Argosy Tours: take a harbor or lake cruise (☎ 206/623-1445; argosycruises.com)
● Beeline Charters & Tours: explore by bus (☎ 206/632-5162; beelinetours.com)

METRO BUSES

● For Metro Rider Information call 206/553-3000 or 206/296-0100; also online information at kingcounty.gov.
● Seventeen bus routes use the Downtown Seattle Transit Tunnel under Pine Street and 3rd Avenue, with five downtown stations: Convention Place, Westlake, University Street, Pioneer Square and the International District. Sunday and evenings after hours, when the tunnel is closed, tunnel buses run above ground (the website gives route information).
● More than 200 other bus routes serve the city and outlying areas. Fares range from $2.50-$3.25 and cash must be put into the farebox next to the driver. You can also purchase a rechargeable ORCA card ($5), valid on buses, trains and ferries in the Puget Sound area. For information, visit orcacard.com.
● Seattle bus drivers are not required to call out the stops along the route. Ask your driver to alert you once you have reached your stop.

LINK LIGHT RAIL

● The Central Link line runs for more than 20 miles (32km), with 16 stations, between the University of Washington and Angle Lake, just southeast of Sea-Tac International Airport.
● Trains run every 6–15 minutes, depending on the day, and fares are $2.25–$3.25 one-way.
● The line is scheduled to be extended 4.5 miles (7.2km) north to Northgate in 2021, with further extensions scheduled for 2024.
● For information, schedules and a trip planner, visit soundtransit.org.

MONORAIL

● The Monorail between Downtown Westlake Center and Seattle Center takes only 2 minutes. Trains run every 5–10 minutes; weekdays 7.30am–11pm and weekends 8.30am–11pm.
● Adult tickets cost $2.50 per ride and can be purchased at Westlake Center and at Seattle Center beneath the Space Needle.
● For details, visit seattlemonorail.com.

SEATTLE STREETCAR

● Although the vintage Waterfront Streetcar has gone, two modern streetcar lines have taken its place. The South Lake Union line connects South Lake Union to Downtown with seven stops, while the First Hill line runs along Capitol Hill to the Chinatown-International District .

● Streetcars run every 10–25 minutes, depending on the day and time, Monday through Sunday, and holidays. Check the website for current schedules. The one-way fare is $2.25 and ORCA cards are accepted.

● For information call 206/553-3000 or visit seattlestreetcar.org.

TAXIS

● Taxis are expensive—get one at your hotel or call for a radio-dispatched cab. Two of the largest and most reputable companies are Yellow Cab (tel 206/622-6500) and Orange Cab (tel 206/522-8800).

● Cab services are busy on Friday and Saturday evenings. Call up to one hour in advance.

● The flag-drop charge is $2.60 and it's $2.70 for each additional mile. Depending on the price of gas at the time, a fuel surcharge may be imposed.

WASHINGTON STATE FERRIES

● Jumbo ferries from Seattle's Downtown terminal to Bainbridge Island and Bremerton (on the Kitsap Peninsula) depart regularly from Colman Dock at pier 52. They take walk-on passengers and cars.

● Most ferry routes are busy during weekday commute periods and on sunny weekends. Expect waits of two hours or more in summer.

● Schedules change seasonally: call 206/464-6400 or visit wsdot.wa.gov/ferries for information.

● Additional ferry routes departing from the Seattle environs serve the Kitsap Peninsula, Vashon Island, Whidbey Island, Port Townsend (Olympic Peninsula), the San Juan Islands and Victoria, British Columbia (Canada).

DISCOUNTS

● The Seattle Visitor Center at the Upper Pike Street Lobby of the Washington State Convention Center offers a complimentary concierge service, including information on discounted tickets for performing arts .
☎ 206/461-5840
🕒 Mon–Fri, and weekends in summer 9–5.

● A CityPass ticket book (valid for nine days) will reduce admission prices by 49 percent to Woodland Park Zoo or Museum of Pop Culture, Space Needle, Pacific Science Center or Chihuly Garden and Glass, Seattle Aquarium and Argosy Cruises Harbor Tour.

● Student travelers are advised to bring a current student ID to obtain discounted admissions.

NEED TO KNOW GETTING AROUND

Essential Facts

MONEY

● Money-changing facilities are available at Sea-Tac Airport and at banks throughout the city.
● Most major establishments and businesses accept major credit and debit cards. Some places will take traveler's checks but few will accept personal checks.
● Automatic Teller Machines (ATMs) are available at banks and throughout the city.

CURRENCY

The unit of currency is the dollar (= 100 cents). Bills (notes) come in denominations of $1, $5, $10, $20, $50 and $100; coins are 25¢ (a quarter), 10¢ (a dime), 5¢ (a nickel) and 1¢ (a penny).

24-HOUR PHARMACIES

● Bartell Drug Store, 600 1st Avenue N (near Seattle Center and several other locations) call 206/284-1354.

ELECTRICITY

● 110 volts, 60 cycles AC current.
● Electrical outlets are for flat, two-prong plugs. European appliances require an adaptor and a converter.

ETIQUETTE

● Seattle dress is informal; for most places, a jacket and tie are optional.
● Seattle has a successful recycling program. Many public places provide recycling bins. Littering is not tolerated.
● Smoking is prohibited in public places.
● Tipping 15–20 percent is customary in restaurants; 15 percent for taxis.

LAVATORIES

Public lavatories are located in Pike Place Market and in the Washington State Convention Center.

LOST PROPERTY

● Airport lost and found (tel 206/787-5312).
● Metro King County lost and found (tel 206/553-3000, online at metro.kingcounty.gov or in person at King Street Center, 201 S Jackson Street).

MAIL

The main Downtown post office is on the corner of Union and 3rd Avenue, open Mon–Fri 8.30–5.30; closed Sat–Sun. Call 800/275-8777 for 24-hour infoline with zip codes, postal rates, post office hours and location; or usps.com. Stamps are sold at many supermarket check-outs.

MEDICAL TREATMENT

● It is vital to have comprehensive insurance.
● US HealthWorks operates several drop-in

clinics; nearest clinic to Downtown is the clinic at 140 4th Avenue N (tel 206/682-7418) open Mon–Fri 7–6, Sat 9–5. Also at 336 NE Northgate Way (tel 206/784-0737) open Mon–Fri 8–6, and 3223 1st Avenue S, Suite C (tel 206/624-3651) open Mon–Fri 6–4.30.
● Dentist Referral Service (tel 206/443-7607); skcds.org.

NATIONAL HOLIDAYS

New Year's Day (Jan 1); Martin Luther King Day (3rd Mon in Jan); President's Day (3rd Mon in Feb); Memorial Day (last Mon in May); Independence Day (Jul 4); Labor Day (1st Mon in Sep); Columbus Day (2nd Mon in Oct); Veterans' Day (Nov 11); Thanksgiving (4th Thu in Nov); Christmas Day (Dec 25).

NEWSPAPERS AND MAGAZINES

● Seattle has one daily printed newspaper: *The Seattle Times* (tel 206/624-7323).
● Free weeklies that provide entertainment listings include the alternative *The Stranger* and *Seattle Weekly*.
● The *Seattle Gay News* is a community newspaper (sgn.org).
● International newspapers are sold at First and Pike News (93 Pike Street at the Pike Place Market) and at Bulldog News (4208 University Way NE).

OPERATING HOURS

● Banks: Generally Mon–Fri 9.30–5, some open Saturdays and Sundays.
● Offices: Normally Mon–Fri 9–5.
● Stores in Downtown open 9–10am and typically close at 5–6pm, with some staying open until 9pm on Thursday evenings. Shops in shopping malls generally stay open Mon–Sat until 9pm; Sun until 5 or 6pm.

POLICE STATIONS

Downtown Seattle's police stations are at 810 Virginia Street and 510 Fifth Avenue. The non-emergency contact number is 206/625-5011.

CONSULATES

● Canadian:
✉ 1501 4th Avenue, Suite 600
☎ 206/443-1777
● French:
✉ 2200 Alaskan Way, Suite 490
☎ 206/256-5184
● Japanese:
✉ 601 Union Street, Suite 500
☎ 206/682-9107

VISITOR INFORMATION

● Seattle Visitor Center and Concierge Services
✉ Upper Pike Street Lobby in the Washington State Convention Center (7th and Pike)
☎ 206/461-5840; visitseattle.org
🕐 Mon–Fri 9–5 year-round; also Sat–Sun 9–5 Memorial Day–Labor Day
● Seattle Center Info
☎ 206/684-7200; seattlecenter.com
● Seattle Public Library offers a Quick Information number
☎ 206/336-4636; spl.org

EMERGENCY PHONE NUMBERS

● Police, ambulance or fire
☎ 911
● The Red Cross Language Bank provides free, on-call interpretive assistance in emergency or crisis situations. Volunteers in more than 60 languages
☎ 206/323-2345

WEIGHTS & MEASURES

Metric equivalents for US weights and measures:
● Weights:
1 ounce (oz) = 28 grams
1 pound (lb) =
0.45 kilogram
1 quart (qt) = 0.9 liter (L).
● Measurements:
1 inch (") = 2.5 centimeters
1 foot (') = 0.3 meter
1 yard (yd) = 0.9 meter
1 mile = 1.6 kilometers

Non-emergency crimes can also be reported online at the seattle.gov website

TELEPHONES
● The area code for Seattle is 206.
● To call Seattle from the UK dial 00 1 (the code for the US), followed by the area code, then the 7-digit number.
● To call the UK from Seattle, dial 011 44 then drop the first zero from the area code.
● To make a local call from a pay phone, listen for a dial tone, then deposit coins; wait for new dial tone and dial the number.
● Phonecards for long-distance calls are available at most shops and some phones take credit cards. To pay cash for long-distance calls, follow the same initial procedure as for local calls, and a recorded operator message will tell you how much additional money to deposit for the first three minutes; then deposit additional coins and dial.
● Directory assistance is a toll call. For information, dial 411 or 1 plus the area code, plus 555-1212.
● Using your cell (mobile) phone abroad can incur hefty roaming charges. Consider having your phone unlocked by your service provider and installing a new SIM card suited to your destination, or pick up an inexpensive pay-as-you-go phone after you arrive. You can also turn off your data roaming, then find a WiFi hot spot and use a service such as Skype, Google Talk or FaceTime.

TELEVISION AND RADIO
● Seattle's two National Public Radio stations (NPR) are KUOW at 94.9 FM (all-talk radio with news from the BBC) and KNKX, an award-winning jazz station, which can be found at 88.5 FM.
● KING-FM (98.1) Classical music.
● Seattle's local TV channels are: KOMO 4 (ABC); KING 5 (NBC); KIRO 7 (CBS); KCTS/9 (PBS); KZJO 22 (MNT/FOX); KFFV 45 (independent).

Culinary Tours

Foodies flock to Seattle to sample the food of some of the nation's most accomplished chefs and innovative restaurateurs. The gourmet pubs, chic bistros and restaurants benefit from the region's dedicated farmers, fishers and artisan food producers. Take a tour to get the best out of your visit.

BON VIVANT WINE TOURS

bonvivanttours.com

In addition to the Woodinville wineries, this company sometimes heads out to places like Bainbridge Island, Yakima or Leavenworth.

☎ 206/524-8687 ⏱ Duration usually 6–7 hours, sometimes longer 💲 $89–$135

SEATTLE BREWERY WALKING TOURS

seattlebrewerywalkingtours.com

Tour three or four breweries in the Ballard and Fremont neighborhoods, all within a mile of each other. Includes four tastings at each brewery and a souvenir. Non-beer options are available.

☎ 206/947-4001 ⏱ Duration 3–3.5 hours 💲 $60–$70

ROAD DOG BREWERY TOURS

roaddogtours.com

This company will be your designated driver on a tour that includes three craft breweries or micro-distilleries. Coffee tours visit several selected coffee shops.

☎ 206/249-9858 ⏱ Duration 2–3 hours 💲 $49–$79

SAVOR SEATTLE FOOD TOURS

savorseattletours.com

Six themed walking tours within Seattle range from a guided stroll around Pike Place Market, with tastings and behind-the-scenes visits, to eating your way around five of the city's finest restaurants (yes, on one tour).

☎ 206/209-5485 ⏱ Times vary. Duration 2 hours 💲 $41.99–$139.99

SEATTLE BITES FOOD TOURS

seattlebitesfoodtours.com

Meet the merchants at Pike Place Market and taste generous portions of food prepared specially for you. You'll also learn about the market's history.

☎ 425/922-9872 ⏱ Duration 2.5 hours 💲 $43.99

ETHNIC SEATTLE FOOD TOURS

ethnicseattle.com

Visit the communities of Little Saigon and Japantown on a family-friendly walking tour that may include a tofu factory, a seafood market, and a local tea shop. Get the insider's knowledge on the city's best dim sum, sushi, and noodles. Tours are seasonal, check the website for current offerings.

☎ 206/628-0994 ⏱ Duration 3 hours 💲 $65

SEATTLE WINE TOURS

seattlewinetours.com

The Woodinville area has more than 100 wineries, and you'll visit some on these luxury customized tours.

☎ 206/444-9463 ⏱ Duration 4 hours to multi-day tours 💲 From $299 for up to four people

EAT SEATTLE

eatseattletours.com

Chef guided small-group food tours of Pike Place Market. Visit the top vendors at the market, learn how to choose the right ingredients for a meal, and indulge in many delicious treats along the way.

☎ 206/653-0537 ⏱ Duration 2 hours 💲 $49

Timeline

CHIEF SEALTH

Sealth was born in 1786 on Blake Island. In 1792, the young boy watched "the great canoe with giant white wings"—Captain Vancouver's brig—sail into Puget Sound. In his twenties he became leader of the Suquamish, Duwamish and allied bands, and became a friend to white settlers. One of these settlers, the pioneer Arthur Denny, suggested changing the settlement's name from Alki to Sealth, which, being difficult for whites to pronounce, was soon corrupted to Seattle. Preceding the Indian War of 1856, Governor Isaac Stevens drafted a settlement promising the native tribes payments and reservation lands. Fearing his people's ways would disappear completely, Sealth reluctantly signed.

Totem poles in Pioneer Square and a memorial to Chief Sealth recall a time when the area was a Suquamish settlement (left, right); a statue of Lenin, Fremont (middle)

1792 British Captain George Vancouver and his lieutenant, Peter Puget, explore the "inland sea," which Vancouver names Puget Sound.

1851 David Denny, John Low and Lee Terry reach Alki Point and found "New York–Alki."

1852 Pioneers move the settlement across Elliott Bay to what is now Pioneer Square.

1853 Henry Yesler opens a steam sawmill, founding the timber industry. President Fillmore signs an act creating the Washington Territory.

1856 The so-called "Indian War": US battle sloop *Decatur* fires into Downtown to root out native peoples, who burn the settlement.

1869 The city is incorporated and passes its first public ordinance—prohibiting drunkenness.

1889 The Great Seattle Fire causes damage exceeding $10 million.

1893 James Hill's Great Northern Railroad reaches its western terminus, Seattle.

1897 The ship *Portland* arrives carrying "a ton of gold" and triggers the Klondike Gold Rush.

1909 The construction of Lake Washington Ship Canal begins, ending in 1917.

1919 The Seattle General Strike—60,000 workers walk off the job.

1940 The Lake Washington Floating Bridge, now the Lacey V. Murrow Memorial Bridge, links Seattle with Eastside communities.

1941 The US enters World War II. Workers flood Seattle to work in the shipyards.

1949 An earthquake measuring 7.2 on the Richter scale strikes the area.

1980 Mount St. Helens erupts, showering ash over Seattle, 100 miles (161km) away.

1999 The World Trade Organization meets in Seattle. Protesters take to the streets.

2001 An earthquake measuring 6.8 causes more than $1billion in damage in Seattle.

2005 Seattle wins the distinction of Most Literate City in the United States.

2013 Construction of the Alaska Way Viaduct replacement tunnel and waterfront improvement plans begin.

2016 Record level high-rise construction as tech companies move into the city again.

2018 The Washington State Convention Center's $1.6 billion expansion begins.

2019 The Museum of Flight receives Apollo 11's command module during the 50th anniversary of the historic mission to the moon.

NEED TO KNOW TIMELINE

CORPORATE HISTORY

- 1970: Boeing's decision to lay off 60,000 workers over a two-year period precipitates a recession.
- 1971: Starbucks opens in Pike Place Market, launching the nation's specialty coffee craze.
- 1975: Bill Gates and Paul Allen start Microsoft.
- 2000: The US Justice Department anti-trust rulings order the breakup of Microsoft. Microsoft appeals.
- 2001: Boeing moves its HQ to Chicago. The Seattle area reels from the dot.com collapse.
- 2013: Boeing records more than $86 billion in sales; its huge manufacturing complex remains the city's largest employer.
- 2014: City announces the phasing in of a minimum wage of $15 per hour, the highest in the US.

Native American art (left, right); the bronze statue of a halibut fisherman that tops the Fishermen's Memorial in the terminal (middle)

Index

Titles in the Series